An Alexander Campbell Reader

An Alexander Campbell Reader

Introduced and Prepared by
Lester G. McAllister

CBP Press
St. Louis, Missouri

CBP Press
Box 179
St. Louis, MO 63166.

Library of Congress Cataloging-in-Publication Data

Campbell, Alexander, 1788-1866.
   [Selections. 1988]
   An Alexander Campbell reader / introduced and prepared by Lester
G. McAllister.
     p. cm.
   Includes index.
   ISBN 0-8272-0017-X : $8.95
   1. Theology. 2. Church and social problems. 3. Restoration
movement (Christianity) 4. Campbell, Alexander, 1788-1866.
5. Christian Church (Disciples of Christ)—Doctrines.
I. McAllister, Lester G. II. Title.
BX7322.C3625 1988
286.6—dc19   88-7352
                                               CIP

Printed in the United States of America

Contents

Introduction

In the year the American constitution was adopted, a child was born in northern Ireland who was destined to influence greatly religious life in the United States and around the world. Alexander Campbell came to this country in 1809 and soon became the major leader of a nineteenth century reformation movement known variously as the Churches of Christ, Christian Churches, and Christian Church (Disciples of Christ).

The bicentennial of Campbell's birth on September 12, 1988 will be celebrated widely. The anniversary will be marked by special lectures (sponsored by the Disciples of Christ Historical Society and several educational institutions) and various other events.

It is thought *An Alexander Campbell Reader*, outlining the important contributions of the man, together with a selection of his writings, will add to that celebration. Such a *Reader* also will help in our appreciation of Campbell's many accomplishments, as well as foster better understanding of our heritage.

No work of this nature can be undertaken without a debt to any number of persons. I should like to express my sincere appreciation in particular to Herbert H. Lambert, who suggested the project; Harold E. Fey, who helped in editing; and David I. McWhirter, Librarian and Archivist of the Disciples of Christ Historical Society, Nashville, and Mary Anne Parrott, Curator of the Discipliana Collection of the Disciples Seminary Foundation, Claremont, for their help with materials.

Lester G. McAllister
Claremont, California
December 1, 1987

Alexander Campbell As a Man of Action

In retrospect, Alexander Campbell (1788-1866) was a man of action. In his long and fruitful life, he produced so many contributions in a number of areas that he became nationally known both within and without Christian circles. Whether it was as preacher, reformer, publisher, or educator, Campbell took the initiative in Christian development on the American frontier. He had the necessary energy and aptitude, combined with self-reliant enterprise and self-initiated activity, to achieve significant results.

Alexander was unlike his father, Thomas Campbell (1763-1854), who spent his formative years in Ireland and Scotland and, therefore, brought to America a continental viewpoint. He was unlike Barton W. Stone (1772-1844), born in America and reared on the frontier. Alexander Campbell came from northern Ireland to the frontier of western Pennsylvania in early manhood while his personality and character were flexible. He was able to combine the best features of his British and his American background.

After marrying Margaret Brown (1791-1827) on March 12, 1811, Campbell and his wife settled on his father-in law's farm in northwestern Virginia (now West Virginia), not far from Washington, Pennsylvania. Along with farming, Alexander concerned himself with the state of Christianity on the frontier. He managed to turn his abundant energies to countless activities, many of which were of benefit to society and the church.

The development of his farm is a story in itself. At first named Lower Buffalo, Campbell soon changed the name to Bethany. His estate grew from 300 acres and a small house to 1,500 or more acres and a larger house of 20 rooms. With money made largely on the farm, Alexander was able to finance his ministry. Later, with his own funds he developed a printing office, founded a college and, in time, a village.

Alexander Campbell's approach involved common sense and reason at a time when emotionalism and revivalism dominated the Christian experience. He believed that the Calvinist's complete dependence upon God was unnecessary and that a special experience of salvation need not be sought. Faith was to be based upon the "reasonableness" of Scripture. Salvation was up to the individual who heard the gospel. A person had only to believe, repent, and obey. It was as clear and as simple as that. His emphasis was upon what individuals could do, an idea that harmonized with the self-reliance of the frontier.

Beginnings

It was a logical impulse which led the Disciples to celebrate their centennial in 1909, Barton W. Stone notwithstanding. The appearance in 1809 of Thomas Campbell's *Declaration and Address* was reason enough. That year also marks the reunion of Alexander and the family with the father, Thomas. They had been separated for more than two years. The son and the father quickly discovered that independently they each had broken relationship with the Presbyterian church and the Reformed tradition. It was obvious they were on a new quest, not knowing where it would lead.

The United States in 1809 just finished its second decade under the constitution. Overpopulation of the coastal areas, widespread unemployment, and the availability of choice lands elsewhere led large numbers of families to move west along the Cumberland Road toward the confluence of the Allegheny and Monongahela rivers at Pittsburgh and through the Cumberland Gap into the bluegrass of central Kentucky.

In a newly settled part of the country, free from the establishments of the eastern shore and the traditions and prejudices of Europe, settlers dreamed of new beginnings. New forms of church life seemed not only possible, but even desirable. In church, as well as in public affairs, laypeople were assuming a larger share of decision-making and governance responsibilities.

When the Campbells arrived on the frontier of western Pennsylvania, the larger proportion of the American people were attached to no church. In the newer western settlements there was a limitless opportunity for evangelization, innovation, and religious experimentation. Seldom before had such conditions of religious freedom existed.

In what was known as the Redstone country of southwestern Pennsylvania, the Methodists, Baptists, and Presbyterians had already established themselves. The Methodists entered the region most recently (in 1780), with the Redstone circuit first appearing in their minutes in 1784. The first congregation of the Baptists dated from 1770. The Presbyterians were at work in the area for the longest time, having arrived in 1766. They formed the Redstone Presbytery in 1781 and were the largest of the three groups serving western Pennsylvania.

Unfortunately, the Presbyterians transplanted all their controversies from the old world to the new. In the Redstone country, most of their divisions were represented. They included the Seceder and the Anti-Seceder, the Reformed and, after 1812, the Associate Reformed as well as the "regular" Presbyterians (that is, those from the Church of Scotland). This complexity was the immediate cause of Thomas Campbell's interest in a way to simplify the relationships between Christian groups by uniting them.

This was the situation that led Thomas, and later Alexander, to advocate some means of Christian union. The Campbells proposed what seemed to them a basis on

11

which to come together: the Scriptures. At that time this platform represented a broad, liberal, and common sense point of view.

Pointing out the widely accepted essentials to faith found in the Scriptures, the Campbells thought they were proposing a plan that would take in everybody. Theirs was not necessarily a new idea, but it was new as far as western Pennsylvania was concerned. Certainly union would strengthen Christian forces on the frontier and aid in evangelization.

It was almost inevitable that there would be a revolt against many of the doctrines of Calvinism. The ground had been laid for such a revolt by the development in Great Britain in the last half of the 18th Century of a number of evangelical groups rediscovering New Testament practice. One far-reaching result of this freedom was the birth of several movements claiming the New Testament as a source of fresh insight into religion.

By the time Alexander Campbell came to western Pennsylvania, such movements had appeared in New England under the leadership of Elias Smith (1769-1846) and Abner Jones (1772-1841), in southern Virginia and North Carolina under the teaching of James O'Kelly (1735?-1826), and in central Kentucky under the preaching of Barton W. Stone (1772-1844). These leaders felt they had made almost identical discoveries of what they considered "a simple faith based on the New Testament." They believed adoption of such a faith would lead to Christian union.

As Thomas and Alexander Campbell in 1809 reflected upon their new homeland, about the most conspicuous feature of American Christianity continued to be its divided state. There were several large denominations and a number of smaller ones. The evangelistic task was awesome since most persons remained outside the church. The division of Christian forces became obvious as denomination competed with denomination. With the principle of separation of church and state written into our constitution, compulsory unity of a state church as it was known in Europe was neither possible nor desirable.

Christian unity was now clearly a matter for Christians to settle among themselves by biblical study, doctrinal discussion, persuasion, and voluntary action. It was under such conditions as these that the Campbells began to consider a movement for the unity of all Christians upon the basis of a restoration of New Testament Christianity. They had hoped, if possible, to complete the reformation of the church begun in the 16th Century by Luther and Calvin. In other words, they proposed nothing less than a 19th Century reformation of the church.

As Emerging Leader

After his arrival in America, Alexander Campbell determined to enter the ministry and give himself to the cause of promoting Christian unity on a scriptural basis. He began at once to study under the direction of his father, Thomas, adding to the knowledge he had gained during a winter's study at Glasgow University. After careful preparation, he preached his first sermon at one of the weekly neighborhood meetings on July 15, 1810, two months before his twenty-second birthday.

Thomas Campbell's *Declaration and Address*, proposing a fellowship of believers formed into a Christian Association of Washington (County) to preach and do other Christian work, had not been widely accepted. By the fall of 1810, it became increasingly evident that the reformation of the churches on the principles Alexander and his father advocated was not progressing.

Early in the next year, 1811, the elder Campbell decided that the association must become an independent church in order to carry out the functions and duties of a Christian fellowship. Therefore, at the next meeting of the association, held on May 4, 1811, the group formed a congregation known as Brush Run Church.

At this same meeting Thomas Campbell was chosen elder and Alexander was licensed to preach the gospel. In forming an independent congregation the group took an important step; if its relations with the former church had been strained before, they were now broken. Contrary to the desire of the founders, they had become a separate movement.

On the first Sunday after organizing as a congregation, the members celebrated the Lord's Supper for the first time. Each week thereafter the people shared the bread and the cup. In a short while a discussion arose concerning baptism. After much study Thomas Campbell led the congregation in declaring that the scriptural form of baptism was immersion and, therefore, that that was what they would teach and practice.

On January 3, 1812 Brush Run Church ordained Alexander Campbell to the ministry. He was 23 years of age. His and Margaret's first child, Jane, was born on March 13, 1812. With her birth, Alexander began to re-study the subject of baptism, with the result that on June 12, 1812, he and Margaret, Thomas and Jane Campbell, and the elder Campbells' daughter, Dorothea, together with two other persons, were immersed in Buffalo Creek by a Baptist minister. The young movement was now committed to *believer's baptism by immersion.*

By taking action in the matter of immersion, young Alexander demonstrated initiative. In the following days and months the leadership of the movement passed almost imperceptibly from Thomas' to Alexander Campbell's hands. As the years passed, Alexander led his followers in developing a definite system of religious thought and practice. A review of the many activities in which this man of action engaged until his death in 1866 will reveal why and how he came to exert such great influence on America's religious life.

As Church Reformer

The adoption of immersion by the "reformers," as they were soon called, erected a barrier between them and the other churches. As most of their religious neighbors were Presbyterians, the clergy, especially, were alarmed at the rejection of infant baptism and of ecclesiastical authority.

Throughout the winter of 1812-1813, the members of Brush Run Church met regularly. It was natural that the adoption of immersion would bring the little group into more friendly relations with the Baptists. There were a number of Baptist congregations along the Monongahela River and in the foothills of the Allegheny Mountains. They had formed the Redstone Baptist Association in 1776 for the purpose of fellowship. In 1812 that association had 33 congregations, 20 ministers, and 1,300 members.

In preaching and visiting across the countryside, Thomas and Alexander Campbell soon became acquainted with various Baptist congregations. Before long, Baptist friends were urging them to join the Redstone association. The Campbells hesitated, as the association required acceptance of the Calvinistic confession of faith used by the Philadelphia Baptist Association (similar to the Westminster Confession of Faith of the Presbyterians). A fatal flaw was that the confession was used as a test of fellowship. It had to be affirmed, or one could not be a member of the church.

They knew the Baptists did not fully agree with their plan to return to New Testament Christianity, but at the same time the Campbells wanted to belong to an identifiable church body. In spite of their misgivings, in September, 1815 they accepted the invitation to join the Redstone Baptist Association, but not before they had prepared a statement indicating their purpose to teach and preach only that which they learned from the Scriptures.

At the August, 1816 meeting of the association held at Cross Creek, not far from Bethany, Alexander Campbell was asked to preach, probably so the Baptists could learn more about him. He chose as his topic a "Sermon on the Law" and based his argument on Romans 8:3, with its emphasis on the distinction between the Old and the New Testaments. The Redstone Baptists tended to accept all Scripture without distinction. In the year the Campbells had been in the association there had been some opposition to them, but after the delivery of this sermon the antagonism became pronounced.

For the next fifteen years Alexander Campbell and his father maintained their relationship with the Baptists, but with mounting tension. From the beginning it was evident they did not regard themselves as fully merged into the Baptist denomination and their sense of special mission did not diminish. During these years the Campbells and their followers became not just "reformers" but "Reforming Baptists" and still later, "Disciples."

Alexander preached before many of the Baptist associations in Pennsylvania, Ohio, Virginia, and Kentucky, urging reform but nearly always creating dissension instead. Many of these associations delivered anathemas against him for his views, resulting in a growing separation of the Baptists and Disciples. By the early 1830s, the Baptists were thoroughly disenchanted with Alexander Campbell. However, the disillusionment worked two ways. In the process of separation the Baptists lost several thousand members and many congregations.

As Iconoclast

In the early 1820s, at a time when Alexander Campbell was being received by many Baptist congregations and associations, he conceived the idea of a monthly magazine which could be circulated widely to further disseminate his "reforming" views. *The Christian Baptist*, published between 1823 and 1830, had the positive message of urging a return to simple faith in and obedience to Christ, which would make possible the unity of Christ's followers, the purification of the church, and the triumph of the Kingdom.

Unfortunately, this would require clearing away the supposed ecclesiastical usurpation of power and unscriptural practices. The need to destroy the "accretions of the centuries" could not be evaded if there was to be a new foundation; so, Alexander Campbell became an iconoclast. He took up his task with a zeal that distressed some

16

of his sympathizers and carried him to lengths of which his own maturer judgment did not even approve.

"Restoration of the ancient order of things" became the ideal, and it was applied rigorously. There were to be no missionary societies because there were none in the early church. Clergy should not be paid a salary but should preach voluntarily. Societies to distribute the Bible were suspect. Whatever practice of the church not validated by scriptural authority must be discontinued. When he later became the responsible leader of congregations trying to cooperate among themselves, he saw some of these matters in a different light.

As Debater

No estimate of Alexander Campbell's leadership is complete without a review of his several debates, a form of public presentation at which he excelled. Debates were favored on the frontier, as they provided a measure of intellectual stimulation and entertainment. Campbell found them an ideal medium for circulating his views and promoting reform.

His first debate took place in June, 1820, with John Walker, a Seceder Presbyterian minister of Mt. Pleasant, Ohio as Campbell's opponent. The question of baptism was at issue. The proceedings of this debate were published in a book entitled *Infant Sprinkling Proved to Be A Human Tradition: Being The Substance of A Debate on Christian Baptism* (Steubenville, Ohio: printed by James Wilson, 1820).

Campbell's second debate was with William L. Maccalla (1788-1859), a "regular" Presbyterian. They decided to have the debate at Washington, near Maysville, Kentucky in October, 1823. Published in 1824 as *A Debate on Christian Baptism* (Buffalo, Va., Campbell and Sala), the volume was widely distributed.

The third debate was with Robert Owen (1771-1858), famous 19th Century social reformer of New Lanark, Scotland and New Harmony, Indiana. It was held at Cincinnati, Ohio in April, 1829 and was published the same year by Alexander Campbell at Bethany as *A Debate on the Evidences of Christianity*. The question at issue was Owen's "Social System," which was thoroughly secular. It provided Campbell with an opportunity to defend the traditional understanding of Christian faith.

By the 1830s, Protestants in the Ohio Valley were alarmed at the increase of Catholic influence, due partly to heavy immigration. Campbell's opponent in his fourth debate was John B. Purcell (1800-1883), Roman Catholic bishop of Cincinnati. The discussion took place in 1837. Campbell staunchly defended the Protestant heritage against Catholicism in *A Debate on The Roman Religion*, published by J. A. James and Company, Cincinnati.

The fifth and last of Campbell's debates was that with Nathan L. Rice (1807-1877), a Presbyterian minister of Paris, Kentucky, on the perennial question of baptism. It was held in Lexington, Kentucky in November, 1843. Henry Clay served as moderator. Entitled *A Debate . . . on The Action, Subject, Design and Administrator of Christian Baptism*, the arguments on both sides were published at Pittsburgh in 1844 by Thomas Carter.

The debates with the Presbyterians over the question of immersion and sprinkling may be passed over as simply typical of the times. They were of no lasting significance. Campbell's defense of Christianity in his debate with Owen, however, and of the Protestant position in his debate with Bishop Purcell, marked him as the great champion of Protestantism on the frontier. These debates gave Campbell a prominence far beyond that of his immediate followers, spreading his fame throughout the country and making his name a household word. While doing little to further the goal of a united church, the debates gave wide dissemination of Campbell's views that called for a return of the churches to New Testament practice.

As Politician

When in 1829 Alexander Campbell heard that a convention was being called to rewrite the Virginia constitution (in which his Brooke county was then located), he decided to run for the office of delegate. Campbell was elected as one of ninety-six state delegates and spent three months in Richmond, the capital, taking a prominent part in the proceedings. Also elected as delegates were James Madison and James Monroe, both former presidents of the United States, and John Marshall, former chief justice of the United States Supreme Court.

Campbell was especially desirous to seek an end to slavery in Virginia, but many of the prominent tidewater landowners were at the convention to oppose the idea. Even with such formidable opposition, Alexander led in the fight for a more democratic government.

The printed proceedings of the convention contain many of Campbell's presentations and speeches. His addresses on the right of suffrage, on the basis of legislative representation, and on the county court system reveal an analytical mind. They also demonstrate Campbell's ability to present his viewpoint clearly and convincingly. Unfortunately, his arguments did not carry the day, and the wealthy landowners won.

As Editor and Publisher

The wide circulation in book form of the Campbell-Walker debate of 1820 opened Alexander's eyes to the power of the press. The result was the previously mentioned monthly magazine, *The Christian Baptist*, appearing in 1823, with Campbell as editor.

In order to expedite the magazine's preparation and to share in any possible profits, Alexander Campbell built a small shop on the banks of Buffalo Creek near the bridge leading to the farm, installed his own presses, and secured a printer. This new venture helped to publicize the movement but never made a profit. It had to be subsidized, costing Campbell about $1,000 a year.

The publication of *The Christian Baptist* gave a forum for the movement and carried articles revealing Alexander's iconoclasm. Considering the difficulties of

19

sparse population and postal service, the paper's circulation was large. Copies of the publication went to nearly all the states, Canada, and even Great Britain. A fundamental change from being critic to advocate of organized Christianity brought about Campbell's closing *The Christian Baptist* after seven volumes.

Recognizing the inevitable separation of the Reformers, or Disciples as they were now called, from the Baptists, and fearing that the name Christian Baptist would be given to the movement, on January 4, 1830, Alexander Campbell began a new journal, *The Millennial Harbinger*. Publication of this monthly paper lasted the rest of Campbell's life and continued until December, 1870. It proved to be the most influential periodical of the Disciples movement throughout all but the last years of publication.

To care for a larger magazine, and to allow other printing to be done, additional presses were ordered and installed in a new building in Bethany village. *The Millennial Harbinger* contained from 48 to 60 pages, so that a year's issue made a sizable book. "Extras," special issues devoted to a single topic of current interest, were distributed free to regular subscribers.

Under the editorship of Campbell the magazine spoke as no other paper could for the movement to unite the church on the basis of New Testament Christianity. Seldom paying its own way, and often subsidized by Campbell, it gave stability and form to the movement. There were several generations of Disciples preachers who lived with a full set of *The Millennial Harbinger* on their bookshelves.

For Alexander Campbell, of primary importance in reading the New Testament was the meaning derived from it. He believed improvements could be made in the wording of the King James Version and decided to publish a revised edition. As the basis for such a new version, Campbell used a translation that had been made and published fifty years earlier by three Scottish scholars: George Campbell (the Gospels), James MacKnight (the epistles), and Philip Doddridge (the book of Acts and Revelation). Alexander compared their work with other translations and with a Greek text. After seeking all possible meanings for a passage, he selected the one he thought the most suitable.

The translation was published under the heading *The Sacred Writings of the Apostles and the Evangelists of Jesus Christ, Commonly Styled the New Testament* (Bethany, Brooke Co., Va.: A. Campbell, 1826). Alexander also made "various emendations" to the earlier work, added a preface to each section, a number of critical notes, and an appendix. The chief reasons given by Campbell for a new version were that modern scholarship had produced a better text, that there was now a more thorough knowledge of the ancient languages than the 17th Century possessed, and that "a living language is continually changing."

Campbell resolved that every word of the Greek should be translated into the best possible English and that none should be merely transliterated. He wrote "immerse," therefore, whenever the older versions used "baptize," and "John the Immerser" for John the Baptist.

Often referred to as "The Living Oracles," the new publication was very popular with Campbell's followers and went through several editions. It was to be expected that such a presentation of the New Testament would arouse opposition, especially in denominations not immersing new believers. Surprisingly, even the Baptists were offended, and in various places led angry crowds in burning copies of the book.

By the 1830s, and after separation from the Baptists, the movement made such progress that requests for a hymnal became numerous. Campbell supplied the market in 1835 by editing and publishing a hymnal entitled, *The Disciples Hymn Book*. The hymnal was supposedly prepared in cooperation with Baron W. Stone and other leaders, but Stone had been consulted only indirectly about the content and not at all about the title. On Stone's protest, the name was changed to *The Christian Hymn Book*.

Over the years the hymnal made substantial profits. Campbell generously shared them with the congregations in states where sales were made. In his last years Campbell gave the copyright to the American Christian Missionary Society. From then until it ceased being published in the last quarter of the 19th Century, the profits aided projects of the society.

Campbell printed other books from time to time. Among them were *The Christian System, in Reference to the Union of Christians and a Restoration of Primitive Christianity, as Plead in the Current Reformation* (Bethany Va.: Printed by A. Campbell, 1839) and *Christian Baptism With Its Antecedents and Consequences* (Bethany, Va.: A. Campbell, 1851). *The Christian System* was a revised version of an earlier publication; both editions were made up of previously published articles.

As Preacher

When Alexander Campbell preached his first sermon that Sunday in July, 1810 the message was so well presented that many in the congregation are supposed to have said, "Why he's a better preacher than his father!" And undoubtedly he was. In his first year he preached 106 sermons. Many of the topics and texts are to be found in the diary containing his *Juvenile Essays on Various Subjects* (Alexander Campbell at Glasgow University, Nashville: Disciples of Christ Historical Society, 1971).

Campbell's sermons were neither exposition of a text nor strictly topical presentations. They were logical in form and well-outlined. Richardson, in his well-known biography of Campbell, thought much of Campbell's power came from his choice of subjects, combined with scriptural authority and broad popular appeal. Campbell is reported to have used a controversial style of delivery. He is said to have used few gestures. On the whole, the hearer had the impression of simplicity.

The effect of his sermons was produced not by emphasis of delivery so much as by the bringing together of ideas, a logical development of thought that resulted in an uplifting of the spirit. It has been said that Alexander

Campbell was not so much a preacher as a preacher's preacher. He became a widely emulated model.

In his valuable *Preaching in the Thought of Alexander Campbell* (Bethany Press, St. Louis, 1954), Granville T. Walker contends that it was Campbell who provided the movement an example of preaching that made it possible for the Disciples to achieve outstanding growth on the rapidly expanding American frontier. Campbell provided the movement with a clear, concise statement of New Testament faith and a rational conception of Christianity, demonstrated in the preaching of the gospel. It was at one and the same time so profound that its implications were inexhaustible and yet so simple that the most humble hearer would be moved deeply.

Campbell's ideal of preaching was to present the claims of Christ with an appeal to reason and common sense. The Bible, containing the word of God, was clear and understandable. It was written for ordinary folks; therefore, ordinary folks could understand it when it was properly presented. Nothing further was needed. This form of preaching, uncommon in an era of emotion-laden revivalism, appealed to a vast number of persons.

As Educator

Alexander Campbell's early interest in education is evidenced by the opening of Buffalo Seminary in 1818 within the first decade of his ministry. His special purpose was to find and educate young men as preachers and leaders of the movement being established. The house Alexander and Margaret had received from her father was enlarged to accommodate the students. He boarded them at his family table and taught them personally, often assisted by his father. Board was $1.50 a week and tuition (including Hebrew and Greek lessons) was $5.00 a quarter.

Buffalo Seminary, however, did not serve the purpose for which it was intended, so was discontinued in 1823. Most of the students preferred business to preaching. Its

23

brief existence, however, stands as a monument to Campbell's early concern for education. At the Campbell home today it is interesting to note the aging wallpaper in the rooms in the cellar, placed there over 170 years ago as Alexander moved his family to the basement to make way for the students on the floors above.

Between 1823 and 1840 Campbell gave much thought to the question of education. The national system of public schools was then in the process of formation. He often lectured on the subject before associations of teachers and other educational groups in various parts of the country. In an important series of articles on "A New Institution" appearing in *The Millennial Harbinger* in 1839 he more fully developed his educational philosophy.

Finally, in 1840 Alexander Campbell secured a charter from the Virginia legislature for a four-year college to be known as Bethany. Greatly admiring Thomas Jefferson's University of Virginia at Charlottesville, Campbell desired to make Bethany as much like that institution in curriculum and student life as possible. He furnished land from his farm for the site of the first buildings, assembled a small but competent faculty, and after the actual opening of the college in 1841 served as president for more than twenty years.

Bethany quickly became the principal place of training for preachers and evangelists of the Disciples movement, the educational center for the laity, and, in many respects, the "mother of colleges" for the Disciples. Several distinguished institutions of higher learning today trace their beginnings to Bethany.

The design of collegiate education for a Christian society was stated by Campbell as follows:

> Bethany College is the only College known to us in the civilized world, founded upon the Bible. It is not a theological school, founded upon human theology, nor a school of divinity, founded upon the Bible; but a literary and scientific institution, founded upon the Bible as the basis of all true science and true learning.

24

●●●●●●●●●●

We, indeed are the only denomination or people that could introduce the Bible into a College, and daily teach it, inasmuch as we care for nothing that is not recognized by every party in Christendom. (*The Millennial Harbinger*, 1850, p. 291 ff.)

The founder's interest in Christian unity led to a provision that the College Hall should be used every Sunday for religious worship and instruction, "to be performed by respectable ministers of various denominations."

From its opening Bethany College rapidly rose to become the most important place for the education of Disciples ministers and laity. Many families sent their sons to Bethany to study with the respected Alexander Campbell. It is not surprising, therefore, to find that the influence of Bethany graduates in the leadership of the Disciples was considerable during the second half of the nineteenth and well into the twentieth century.

As Biblical Scholar

In addition to serving as president of the college, Campbell, as professor, regularly gave a series of morning Bible lectures, together with lectures on other subjects, which achieved fame among the students. His scholarship was thorough in biblical studies and in the history and thought of Christianity. There is evidence that he read and was familiar with most of the current scholarship on these subjects published in Great Britain, as well as in the United States.

Alexander Campbell's contribution to biblical interpretation, through the application of historical criticism, began in 1816 with the preaching of the "Sermon on the Law" for the Redstone Baptist Association. In that sermon he asked Christians to adhere to the New Testament as a rule of life and stated that the teachings of Jesus and the apostles, not the laws of Moses, are to be the principal authorities for Christians.

Campbell always considered the New Testament as the Christian's main textbook and argued that it should be read with an open mind. He insisted that every individual should have the right to interpret the Scriptures. When interpreting any book of the Bible, the reader should consider the following circumstances: the author, date, place and occasion of writing, and the person to whom the material was addressed. It is significant that Alexander was willing, at this early date, to apply such methods to the interpretation of the Bible. He saw the Bible as full of the experiences of people struggling to overcome difficulties and seeking to achieve a greater knowledge of God and of God's will.

Campbell was active in the American and Foreign Bible Society, but in 1850 when a group withdrew to form the American Bible Union he joined the new group. During the winter of 1854 and the early part of 1855, he was working on a revision of the book of Acts assigned to him by the Bible Union. It was published in 1855 as a part of a new version of the Bible.

As Public Speaker

Campbell's prominence as leader of a religious movement and as president of a college led to invitations to give lectures before audiences of other colleges, universities, and learned societies. He spoke on a variety of subjects. One was "The Anglo-Saxon Language: Its Origin, Character, and Destiny" (a lecture still being used as late as 1960 in the graduate school of the University of California, Berkeley). Other subjects were: "Address on Capital Punishment," "Address on the Amelioration of the Social State," and "Responsibilities of a Man of Genius." Usually these lectures were carefully worked-out systems of thought. Many of them were published together in a volume entitled, *Popular Lectures and Addresses* (Philadelphia: James Challen and Son, 1863).

As Organizer

Early in the 1840s Campbell's followers increasingly were raising questions about organizations such as conventions and missionary societies. Were they or were they not scriptural? In 1842 Alexander came out in the *Harbinger* with a well-developed rationale for a national organization.

When a convention was finally called to meet in Cincinnati, Ohio, October 22-27, 1849, Alexander Campbell did not find it possible to attend. Whether it was from an illness or, more likely, from a desire to see from afar how it developed, we will never know. In any event, he was elected president and regularly thereafter was re-elected president both of the convention and of the American Christian Missionary Society, which the convention brought into existence, until his death in 1866.

Although attacked vigorously by those who were suspicious of conventions and missionary societies, Campbell continued to advocate them. In fact, he wrote a lengthy series of articles in *The Millennial Harbinger* stressing the necessity for both state and general conventions. He thought of conventions as necessary for fellowship, inspiration, and the transaction of the business of the larger church.

As Social Reformer

Alexander Campbell saw social reform as one of the fruits of church reform. In fact, he viewed the reformation of the churches on a New Testament basis as an indispensable prerequisite for a new social order. He believed that only through the church would it be possible to strike at the roots of social injustice, and that success would be delayed until there was a united church. In short, a united church made possible by the return to New Testament Christianity would bring about the transformation of the social order.

27

Campbell became impatient, however, and found it difficult to wait for the achievement of a united church. He began writing about and speaking out on several of the current issues. He had something to say on temperance, capital punishment, public schools, slavery, and war. He expressed his opinions most fully on the injustice of slavery and the evils of war, the two most pressing issues of the day.

On the question of temperance societies and the prohibition of alcoholic beverages, Campbell at first indicated his opposition, feeling that personal liberty and moral choice were at stake. Within a short while, however, he reversed his position and became an active advocate of prohibition. He believed that divine authority obligated the state to use capital punishment only for the crime of murder. He was a strong supporter of the growing public school movement as a means of creating a prosperous nation, developing a population that would be morally strong and that through reading would know the Bible and God's will.

By the 1840s many Americans realized that the issue of slavery would be increasingly divisive in the life of the nation. The subject was so explosive that friends and families were divided, congregations split, and major denominations separated into North and South. Along with these tensions was the threat of turning to arms to settle the question. Campbell realized he was dealing with emotion-filled issues. Nevertheless, he boldly declared his convictions.

At the Virginia constitutional convention of 1829 in which he participated, and again in 1849, in a tract widely circulated in Kentucky, Campbell proposed a plan for the gradual emancipation of slaves. Within the pages of *The Millennial Harbinger* he wrote a number of editorials and essays on the subject of slavery.

From his writings it is clear Campbell equated morality with a literal interpretation of the New Testament. His father, Thomas, after an exhaustive study of the Bible, discovered that there was no direct condemnation of slavery in either the Old or the New Testaments. The

Campbells, therefore, came to the conclusion that slavery was not immoral. Even though he was strongly against it personally, he believed Christians had no scriptural basis for pronouncing slavery as morally wrong. At the same time, Alexander insisted that Christians ought to treat their slaves as fellow human beings and not as property. He declared that slavery as then practiced was a serious violation of human rights.

Campbell also recognized that slavery was not consistent with the American understanding of freedom. Furthermore, in his opinion, slave labor was detrimental to the economy of the South. To the detriment of his own financial interest, he carried his convictions about slavery into his personal life by freeing every slave he owned or over whom he had control. He passed no judgment, however, on those who failed to follow his example, and Campbell continued to propose the gradual emancipation of slaves.

In keeping with his belief that the Christian community should be all-inclusive, Campbell held firmly to the idea that the ownership of slaves should not be a matter of church discipline or a test of fellowship. To this end he published a famous editorial stating that "Slavery is a matter of opinion," meaning that whether one held slaves or not was not an essential of faith.

As tensions over the issue of slavery mounted, far-reaching minds could see that more and more there was the possibility that the North and South would resort to force to settle the issue. Anticipating this eventuality, Alexander Campbell took an unequivocal stand against war. He had opposed the Mexican War and had much to say against war in *The Millennial Harbinger*.

His fullest statement on the subject was given before the Wheeling, Virginia (now West Virginia) Lyceum in May, 1848, three months after the close of the Mexican War. So powerful was his argument against war that Congressman Joseph B. Shannon of Missouri had it read into the Congressional Record of November 22, 1937, as some leaders saw the United States moving inexorably toward World War II.

In this address Campbell argued that war, though sanctioned and practiced in the Old Testament, is outlawed by both the letter and the spirit of the New Testament, especially in the teachings of Christ. Therefore, he held that no Christian can ever conscientiously sanction or engage in war. Those who would rationalize that a distinction should be made between a defensive and an offensive war Campbell dismissed as quibblers. He believed firmly that war cannot be a means of establishing justice and that it does not end controversy.

Since finally it is around a peace table and not on a battlefield that a war is settled, he figured why not do this before the tragic loss of lives and resources rather than after? He made the proposal that there be a federation of nations and a world court that would settle international disputes, similar to what the United Nations and World Court does today.

Alexander Campbell was truly an uncompromising pacifist. He stated that those persons who follow Christ, like those in the early church, should refuse to fight. Christians should use every effort and all their persuasive powers to get nations to sit down together and work out their difficulties.

Disciples today who wish to make application of the Christian gospel to contemporary social issues may take comfort in knowing that they are in accord with the spirit of Alexander Campbell. He dared to apply that which he found in the New Testament, as he saw it, to the major issues of morality and justice of his day.

As Theologian

Campbell believed that theology, as developed into systems by church leaders throughout the centuries, had corrupted the church. Since he and his followers were trying to return the church to New Testament practice, it was essential that they simply read the Scriptures and accept as doctrine and practice that which was taught in them. Theology as such had no direct place in Campbell's plan of unity on a scriptural basis.

Campbell did not consider himself a theologian, but believed strongly in individual judgment on doctrinal questions, based on a study of scriptures. Nevertheless, much as he disliked the word *theology*, by the nature of his work and ministry Campbell had to deal with it.

Since Alexander Campbell's theology is a major study in and of itself, it is not possible to consider it fully in this short essay. Royal Humbert has collected Campbell's thought from numerous articles, essays, debates, lectures, and other writings and has presented in a sizable volume the substance of Campbell's theology. In *A Compend of Alexander Campbell's Theology* (St. Louis: Bethany Press, 1961), we find Campbell's views on faith and reason, God, Christ, the Holy Spirit, the Bible, revelation, the church, eschatology, and a host of other theological questions.

A Final Word

The picture of Alexander Campbell as a man of action raises the question as to how one man could manage to do so much in the same 24-hour day available to us. The answer lies, of course, in long work days and a disciplined use of time. He regularly rose at four o'clock in the morning and worked until midnight. He varied his activities from preparing text for his printers, to entertaining guests, to reading. Always, morning and evening he held devotions for himself, his family, and all who were in his house.

In addition to preaching, teaching, traveling, writing, and editing, Campbell still found time for managing his farms and considerable estate. Mrs. Selina Campbell, Alexander's second wife, spoke of the broad interests of her husband in her book, *Home Life and Reminiscences of Alexander Campbell by His Wife* (St. Louis: John Burns, 1882). She reported that Campbell took an interest in the public welfare, in the improvement of the roads, and in husbandry. She offered as examples his efforts in building the road to Wellsburg and the development of flocks of sheep that were among the finest in the area.

Alexander's interests really knew no bounds. Campbell was always offering hospitality to a wide range of visitors, both the famous and the less well-known. The Campbell home became a resort for the young and old, family and friends, for those who lived nearby and those from afar. Once, Campbell took an Indian boy from the Iowa tribe, kept him for eight or nine years, and gave him an education. Afterward the boy returned home to help his people. On another occasion a Mexican general of some importance stayed a while with Campbell and later sent two sons to Bethany College.

Alexander Campbell devoted his life to implementing and amplifying the ideas of his father, Thomas. They were best expressed in the *Declaration and Address*, a document that was, in a sense, an American religious declaration of independence. Just as Thomas Jefferson a few years before had challenged the people of a new republic to an adventure in self-government, the Campbells challenged them to a like adventure in Christian development.

Christians were to throw off the encumbrances of the past, the ancient quarrels of Europe, and move to the unity, liberty, simplicity, and purity of the apostolic church. From both the lecture platform and the editor's chair, Alexander Campbell considered every concern of humankind related to Christian faith.

Campbell would see no cause to despair if he were to view the infinite complexities of our society. Even as we give up our too-easy optimism and our belief that society can completely regenerate itself by its agencies of education, technology, economic management and government, Alexander would have us return to that which is taught in the New Testament.

As have Christians throughout the centuries, Campbell realized that our only security lies in the conquest of our sinful nature and the development of our spiritual life. He believed we must ultimately rely upon the grace of God. His faith, based firmly on New Testament promises, rested secure in God's continuing purposes. Alexander Campbell was a man of action working with God to accomplish those purposes.

There are many sources available for knowledge of Alexander Campbell's life and action. Among the most helpful ones are Robert Richardson's *Memoirs of Alexander Campbell* (Philadelphia: J. Lippincott, 1868, 1870); D. Ray Lindley's *Apostle of Freedom* (St. Louis: Bethany press, 1958); Harold L. Lunger's *The Political Ethics of Alexander Campbell* (St. Louis: Bethany press, 1954); and Perry E. Gresham, editor, of *The Sage of Bethany: A Pioneer in Broadcloth* (St. Louis: Bethany press, 1960). Another source is found in the major articles on Campbell appearing from time to time in such magazines as *The Gospel Advocate, The Christian Standard, The Christian-Evangelist* and *The Disciple.*

On the pages that follow are selections from Campbell's writings. They have been edited for the sake of brevity and the modern reader's desire for concise prose. These selections of relevant and better-known writings will each be introduced by a brief statement giving the setting and occasion of the piece.

1810

Alexander Campbell's earliest published writing was a series of essays printed in a weekly newspaper, *The Reporter*, in Washington, Pennsylvania. Essay Number Seven, printed on June 28, 1810, was a strong statement censuring the habit of local young men engaging in profane swearing. (From Richardson's *Memoirs of Alexander Campbell*, Vol. I, pp. 292-293).

On Profane Swearing

When I am addressing you on this subject, I would also make a few observations on another more fashionable vice among our young fops (I cannot call them gentlemen), who are guilty of this horrid vice—I mean, swearing in company with ladies and persons of a moral deportment, to whom this vice is most offensive and abominable.

I say, I cannot call swearers gentlemen, however else qualified; for, says a judicious writer, with whom I precisely agree in this sentiment, "Those who addict themselves to swearing and interlard their discourse with oaths; can never be considered as gentlemen; they are generally persons of low education and are unwelcome in what is called good company. It is a vice that has no temptation to plead, but is, in every respect, as vulgar as it is wicked."

Of all the vices which have ever disgraced human nature; of all the extremes of madness and folly to which mankind has ever run; of all the irreverent, irreligious deeds which have ever blackened human character, there is none more horrid, flagrant or profane; none so presumptuous, arrogant and irreverent, as carelessly, heedlessly and impiously to invoke the sacred name of Him whom angels worship, saints adore, and before whom devils and wicked men shall tremble with horror, anguish and dismay—to invoke the sacred majesty of heaven on every light, frivolous and wicked occasion—to call God to witness every lewd, base, mean or trivial action they perform or perpetrate; and, still worse, to supplicate that pure and righteous Being to damn, curse or punish a fellow-creature, a fellow immortal, or, it may be, some brute or inanimate thing.

And what renders this vice most oppressive to them who are provoked at it is, that our profligate, immoral beaux make it a point to swear the harder if there be any pious persons or ladies in company, thinking to mortify the former and expecting to commend their gallantry to the latter. Be assured, you detestable wretches, that this vice is as degrading to yourselves as it is hateful to others; and there is not a lady who possesses a spark of virtue but will shun and detest your company.

•••••••••••

In short, I know no reason for or temptation to this vice, above all the vices prevalent in the world. Ask a man why he swears, he tells you it is a bad custom he has learned—he cannot quit it. Experience sufficiently proves that it is in the power of any person who makes the attempt to give it over, only let him be determined and watchful.

1816

This famous sermon was preached on September 1, 1816 at the Redstone Baptist Association meeting on Cross Creek, not far from Bethany, when Campbell was twenty-seven years old. Later, Campbell said that it was the controversy which arose over this sermon that encouraged him to promote "the present reformation." The sermon is here greatly abridged but every attempt has been made to present the preacher's main points. (Campbell later published his sermon in a pamphlet and reprinted it in *The Millennial Harbinger*, Series III, Vol.III, September, 1846, pp. 493ff.)

The Sermon on the Law

Text: "For what the law could not do, in that it was weak through the flesh; God, sending his own Son, in the likeness of sinful flesh, and for sin, condemned sin in the flesh" Romans 8:3.

Words are signs of ideas or thoughts. Unless words are understood, ideas or sentiments can neither be communicated nor received. Words that in themselves are quite intelligible may become difficult to understand in different connections and circumstances. One of the most important words in our text is of easy signification, and yet, in consequence of its diverse usages and epithets, it is sometimes difficult precisely to ascertain what ideas should be attached to it.

It is the term *law*. But a close investigation of the context, and a general knowledge of the Scriptures, every difficulty of this kind may be easily surmounted.

In order to elucidate and enforce the doctrine contained in this verse, we shall scrupulously observe the following method.

1. We shall endeavor to ascertain what ideas we are to attach to the phrase *"the law,"* in this and similar portions of the sacred Scriptures.

2. Point out those things which *the law* could not accomplish.

3. Demonstrate the reason why *the law* failed to accomplish those objects.

4. Illustrate how God has remedied those relative defects of *the law*.

5. In the last place, deduce such conclusions from these premises, as must obviously and necessarily present themselves to every unbiased and reflecting mind.

In discussing the doctrine contained in our text, we are, then, in the first place, to endeavor to ascertain what ideas we are to attach to the term *"the law"* in this and similar portions of the sacred Scriptures.

The term *"law"* denotes in common usage, "a rule of action." It was so used by the Jews, until the time of our Saviour, to distinguish the whole revelation made to the patriarchs and prophets from the traditions and commandments of the rabbis or doctors of the law.

The addition of the definite article . . . alters the signification or at least determines it. During the life of Moses, the words *"the law"* without some explicative addition, were never used. Joshua, Moses' successor, denominates the writings of Moses, "the book of the law"; but never uses the phrase by itself. Nor, indeed, have we any authentic account of this phrase being used without some restrictive definition, until the reign of Abijah (2 Chron. 14:4), at which time it is used to denote the whole legal dispensation by Moses. In this way it is used about thirty times in the Old Testament, and as often with such epithets as show that the whole law of Moses is intended.

When the doctrines of the reign of Heaven began to be preached, and to be contrasted in the New Testament with the Mosaic economy, the phrase, *"the law,"* became very common, and when used without any distinguished epithet or restrictive definition, invariably denoted the whole legal or Mosaic dispensation. In this acceptation it occurs about one hundred and fifty times in the New Testament.

I say the *whole* law, or dispensation by Moses; for in modern times the law of Moses is divided and classified under three heads, denominated the moral, ceremonial, and judicial law. This division of the law being unknown to the apostolic age, and of course never used by the apostles, can serve no valuable purpose in obtaining a correct knowledge of the doctrine delivered by the apostles respecting the law.

Hence it is that modern teachers, by their innovations concerning law, have perplexed the student of the Bible, and cause many a fruitless controversy. . . . It does not militate with this statement to grant that some of the precepts of the Decalogue have been repromulgated by Jesus Christ.

Before dismissing this part of the subject, we would observe that there are two principles, commandments, or laws that are never included in our observations respecting the law of Moses, nor are they ever in Holy Writ called the law of Moses; these are, "Thou shalt love the Lord thy God with all thy heart, soul, mind, and strength; and thy neighbor as thyself." These our Great Prophet teaches us, are the basis of the law of Moses, and of the prophets.

Let it, then, be remembered, that in the Scriptures, these precepts are considered the basis of all law and prophesy; consequently when we speak of the law of Moses we do not include these commandments, but that whole modification of them sometimes called the legal dispensation.

We shall now attempt to point out those things which *the law* could not accomplish.

In the first place, it could not give righteousness and life. Righteousness and eternal life are inseparably connected.

Where the former is not, the latter can not be enjoyed. Whatever means puts us in possession of one puts us in possession of the other.

But this the law could not do. "For if there had been a law given which could have given life, verily, righteousness should have been by the law" (Gal. 3:21). "If righteousness comes by the law, then Christ is dead in vain." These testimonies of the Apostle, with the whole scope of divine truth, teach us that no man is justified by the law, that righteousness and eternal life cannot be received through it.

In the second place, the law could not exhibit the malignity or demerit of sin. It taught those that were under it, that certain actions were sinful—to these sinful actions it gave descriptive names—one is called theft, a second murder, a third adultery. It showed that these actions were offensive to God, hurtful to men, and deserved death. But how extensive their malignity and vast their demerit the law could not exhibit. This remained for later times and other means to develop.

In the third place, the law could not be a suitable rule of life to mankind in this imperfect state. It could not be a rule to all mankind, as it was given to and designed only for a part. It was given to the Jewish nation, and to none else.

Do we not know, with Paul, that what things soever the law saith, it saith to them that are under the law? But even to the Jews it was not the most suitable rule of life. "Tis universally agreed that example, as a rule of life, is more influential than precept. Now the whole Mosaic law wanted a model or example of living perfection." The most exemplary characters under the law, had their notable imperfections.

And as long as polygamy, divorces, slavery, revenge, etc., were winked at under that law, so long must the lives of its best subjects be stained with glaring imperfections.

But we hasten to the third thing proposed in our method, which is to demonstrate the reason why the law could not accomplish these objects.

The Apostle in our text briefly informs us that it was owing to human weakness that the law failed to accomplish these things—"In that it was weak through the flesh." The defects of the law are of a relative kind. . . . It is not in itself weak or sinful—some part of it was holy, just and good—other parts of it were elementary, shadowy, representations of good things to come. If the law had been faultless, no place should have been found for the gospel.

We have now arrived at the fourth head of our discourse, in which we propose to illustrate the means by which God has remedied the relative defects of the law.

All those defects the Eternal Father remedies by sending his own Son, in the likeness of sinful flesh, and for sin, condemns sin in the flesh.

He magnifies the law, and makes it honorable. All this he achieves by his own obedience unto death. He finished the work which the Father gave him to do; so that in him all believers, all the spiritual seed of Abraham, find righteousness and eternal life; not by legal works or observances, in whole or in part, but through the abundance of grace, and the gift of righteousness, which is by him—"For the gift of God is eternal life through Jesus Christ our Lord."

That which remains . . . is to show how the failure of the law, in not being a suitable rule of life, has been remedied.

We noticed that example is a more powerful teacher than precept. Now Jesus Christ has afforded us an example of human perfection never witnessed before. He gave a living form to every moral and religious precept which they never before possessed.

It now remains in the last place, to deduce such conclusions from the above premises, as must obviously and necessarily present themselves to every candid and reflecting mind.

First. From what has been said, it follows that there is an essential difference between law and gospel—the Old Testament and the New.

No two words are more distinct in their signification than *law* and *gospel.* They are contra-distinguished under various names in the New Testament.

Second. In the second place, we learn from what has been said, that "there is no condemnation to them which are in Christ Jesus." The premises from which the Apostle drew this conclusion are the same with those stated to you in this discourse. "Sin," says the Apostle, "shall not have dominion over you; for ye are not under the law, but under grace." In the sixth and seventh chapters to the Romans, the Apostle taught them that "they were not under the law," that "they were freed from it"—"dead to it"—"delivered from it."

Third. In the third place, we conclude from the above premises that there is no necessity for preaching the law in order to prepare men for receiving the gospel.

This conclusion perfectly corresponds with the commission given by our Lord to the Apostles, and with their practice under that commission. "Go," saith he, "into all the world, and preach the gospel unto every creature." "Teach the disciples to observe all things whatsoever I command you." Thus they were authorized to preach the gospel, not the *law*, to every creature. Thus they were constituted ministers of the New Testament, not of the Old.

. . . in the whole history of primitive preaching, we have not one example of preaching the law as preparatory to the preaching or reception of the gospel.

Fourth. A fourth conclusion, which is deductible from the above premises, is that all arguments and motives, drawn from the law or Old Testament, to urge the disciples of Christ to baptize their infants; to pay tithes to their teachers; to observe holy days or religious fasts, as preparatory to the observance of the Lord's Supper; to sanctify the seventh day; to enter into national covenants; to establish any form of religion by civil law—and all reasons and motives borrowed from the Jewish law to

41

excite the disciples of Christ to a compliance with or an imitation of Jewish customs, are inconclusive, repugnant to Christianity, and fall ineffectual to the ground; not being enjoined or countenanced by the authority of Jesus Christ.

Fifth. In the last place we are taught, from all that has been said, to venerate in the highest degree the Lord Jesus Christ; to receive him as the Great Prophet, of whom Moses, in the law, and all the prophets did write. To receive him as the Lord of our righteousness, and to pay the most punctilious regard to all his precepts and ordinances.

Let every one that nameth the name of Christ depart from all iniquity. Let us walk worthy of him. Let us take heed lest by our conduct we should represent Christ as the minister of sin. Let us not walk after the flesh but the Spirit; and then we shall show that the righteousness of the law is fulfilled in us. Then shall no occasion be given to the adversary to speak reproachfully. And if any should still urge the stale charge of Antinomianism, or affirm that we lived in sin that grace might abound; did evil that good might come; or made void the law through faith; let us put to silence the ignorance of foolish men, by adoring the doctrine we profess with a blameless conduct. . . .

May he that hath the key of David, who openeth and no man shutteth, and shutteth and none can open, open your hearts to receive the truth in the love of it, and incline you to walk in the light of it, and then ye shall know that the ways thereof are pleasantness, and all the paths thereof are peace! *Amen.*

1823

On July 4, 1823 at Buffalo, Virginia (now Bethany, West Virginia), Alexander Campbell issued the first number of a new publication in which he hoped to attract the attention of all persons seeking truth in religion. The following selection, taken from the "Preface," is presented to help in understanding something of the spirit and vision of the young editor. (From *The Christian Baptist*, Vol. I, No. 1, July 4, 1823).

Preface to *The Christian Baptist*

We now commence a periodical paper, pledged to no religious sect in Christendom, the express and avowed object of which is the eviction of truth and the exposure of error. We expect to prove whether a paper perfectly independent, free from any controlling jurisdiction except the bible, will be read; or whether it will be blasted by the poisonous breath of sectarian zeal and of an aspiring priesthood. As far as respects ourselves, we have long since afforded such evidence as would be admitted in most cases, of the disinterested nature of our efforts to propagate truth, in having always declined every pecuniary inducement that was offered, or that could have been expected.

•••••••••••

This paper shall embrace a range of subjects and pursue a course not precisely similar to those of any other periodical work which we have seen. Of this, however, the work itself will give the plainest and most intelligible exhibition. In introducing facts and documents in support of assertion or demonstration, there is a possibility of adducing such as are not true or genuine, owing to a variety of causes. Of this indeed, we shall be always on our guard. If, however, on any occasion any thing should be exhibited as fact which is not fact, we pledge ourselves to give publicity to any statement, decently written, tending to disprove any such alleged facts.

••••••••••

It is very far from our design to give any just ground of offence to any, the weakest of the disciples of Christ, nor to those who make no pretensions to the Christian name; yet we are assured that no man ever yet became an advocate of that faith which cost the life of its founder and the lives of so many of the friends and advocates of it, that did not give offence to some. . . . We have only one request of our readers—and that is, an impartial and patient hearing; for which we shall make them one promise, viz. that we shall neither approve nor censure any thing without the clearest and most satisfactory evidence from reason and revelation.

Dedication

To all those, without distinction, who acknowledge the Scriptures of the Old and New Testaments to be a Revelation from God; and the New Testament as containing the Religion of Jesus Christ:

Who, willing to have all religious tenets and practices tried by the Divine Word; and who feeling themselves in duty bound to search the Scriptures for themselves, in all matters of Religion, are disposed to reject all doctrines and commandments of men, and to obey the truth, holding fast the faith once delivered to the Saints—this work is most respectfully and affectionately dedicated by

The Editor

1823

Much that Campbell wrote in *The Christian Baptist* was the work of an iconoclast. In the light of New Testament teaching he questioned many of the contemporary practices such as sending out missionaries from denominational organizations. The following selection is typical of his comments. (From *The Christian Baptist*, Vol. I, No. 2, September 1, 1823, pp. 14-17).

Concerning Modern Missionary Schemes

The seventy disciples, who were sent out by the Messiah to go before his face, and to announce the approaching reign, were sent, in the same manner, empowered to confirm their testimony by signs and wonders. See Luke X. The apostles, in the last commission, were sent to all the world; but were prohibited, in the accompanying instructions, from commencing their operations, until they should be endued with a power on high. Thus all the missionaries, sent from heaven, were authorized and empowered to confirm their doctrine with signs and wonders sufficient to awe opposition, to subdue the deepest rooted prejudices, and to satisfy the most inquisitive of the origin of their doctrine.

•••••••••

The success of all modern missionaries is in accordance with these facts. . . . As the different philosophers, in ancient nations, succeeded in obtaining a few disciples to their respective systems, each new one making some inroads upon their predecessors; so have the modern missionaries succeeded in making a few proselytes to their systems, from amongst the disciples of the different pagan systems of theology. But that any thing can be produced, of a credible character, resembling the success of the divine missionaries, narrated in the New Testament, is impossible; or, that a church, resembling that at Jerusalem, Samaria, Cesaria, Antioch, or Rome, has been founded in any pagan land, by the efforts of our missionaries, we believe incapable of proof. Is, then, the attempt to convert the heathen by means of modern missionaries, an unauthorized and a hopeless one? It seems to be unauthorized, and, if so, then it is a hopeless one.

Missionaries to Burmah

On Wednesday, the 11th of June, at Utica, New York, the Rev. Jonathan Wade and his consort were set apart as missionaries to the Burmah empire, by a committee of the board of managers of the Baptist General Convention. An interesting sermon was delivered on the occasion by the Rev. Nathaniel Kendrick. . . . Rev. Alfred Bennett led in offering up the consecrating prayer. Rev. Daniel Hascall gave Mr. Wade an appropriate charge and the Rev. Joel W. Clark gave him the right hand of fellowship. . . . The services were performed in Rev. Mr. Atkins' meeting-house. . . .

Note by the Editor—It is much to be desired that the Baptists in the western country will not imitate these precedents of pompous vanity, so consecrated in the east; and that they will rather cherish the spirit and copy the style of that much despised little volume called the New Testament. Then we know they will remember that it is spoken by our Lord, "Be not called Rabbi," or Reverend. Then they will confess that many things of high reputation in this age are an abomination in the sight of God.

46

1823

One of Campbell's favorite means of getting his ideas across came in replying to "Letters to the Editor." In one such reply he takes occasion to show his disapproval of Bible societies. Campbell's change of heart in regard to such societies was demonstrated by his cooperation with the American Bible Union in the 1850s. (From *The Christian Baptist*, Vol. I, No. 5, December 1, 1823)

Concerning Bible Societies

Sir: Yours of the 6th instant came duly to hand. I am obliged to you for its contents. You think that it was rather going to an extreme to rank bible societies with other popular schemes. Perhaps a more intimate acquaintance with our views of Christianity would induce you to think as we do upon this subject. We are convinced, fully convinced, that the whole head is sick, and the whole heart faint of modern fashionable Christianity—that many of the schemes of the populars resemble the delirium, the wild fancies of a subject of fever. . . . We admit that it is quite as difficult to convince the populars of the folly of their projects, as it generally is to convince one in a febrile reverie, that he is not in the possession of his reason. . . .

With regard to bible societies, they are the most specious and plausible of all the institutions of this age. No man who loves the Bible can refrain from rejoicing at its increasing circulation. But every Christian who understands the nature and design, the excellence and glory of the institution called the Church of Jesus Christ, will lament to see its glory transferred to a human corporation. The church is robbed of its character by every institution, merely human, that would ape its excellence and substitute itself in its place. . . . Let every church of Christ, then, if it can only disseminate twenty bibles or twenty testaments in one year, do this much. Then it will know into what channel its bounty flows; it will need no recording secretary, no president, no managers of its bounty. It will send all this pageantry, this religious show, to the regions of pride and vanity, whence they came. Then the church and its king will have all the glory.

Your friend,
The Editor

1824

Campbell spent quite a few issues of *The Christian Baptist* chastising the clergy for their arrogance, pride and lack of commitment. In the following selection he suggests that much of the problem relates to the material demands of the clergy. If they would only preach for the love of the Lord, and earn their living elsewhere, a "purer" church would emerge. Campbell later modified his views on this as well as other subjects. (From *The Christian Baptist*, Vol. I, No. 7, February 2, 1824, pp. 42-46)

Concerning a Paid Clergy

Money, I think, may be considered not merely as the bond of union in popular establishments, but it is really the rock on which the popular churches are built. Before church union is proposed, the grand point to ascertain is, are we able to support a church? Before we give a call, let us see, says the prudent saint, what we can "make up." A meeting is called—the question is put, "how much will you give?" It goes round. Each man writes his name or makes his mark. A handsome sum is subscribed. A petition is sometimes presented to the legislature for an act of incorporation to confirm their union and to empower them to raise by the civil law, or the arm of power, the stipulated sum. All is now secure. The church is founded upon this rock. It goes into operation. The parson comes. Their social prayers, praises, sacraments, sermons and fasts commence; every thing is put into requisition. But what was the *primum mobile*? What the moving cause? Money. As proof of this, let the congregation decrease by emigration or death; the money fails; the parson takes a missionary tour; he obtains a louder call; he removes. Money failed is the cause; and when this current freezes, social prayers, praises, "sacraments," sermons, and congregational fasts all cease. Money, the foundation, is destroyed, and down comes the superstructure raised upon it. Reader, is not this fact? And dare you say that money is not the basis of the modern religious establishments? It begins with money; it goes on with money, and it ends when money fails. Money buys Aesop's fables for the destined priest; money consecrates him to office, and a moneyed contract unites him and his parish. The church of Jesus Christ is founded upon another basis, nourished by other means, is not dissolved by such causes, and will survive all the mines of Peru, all the gold of Ophir. The modern clergy say they do not preach for money. Very well; let the people pay them none, and they will have as much of their preaching still. Besides, there will be no suspicion of their veracity.

1826

The following selections are taken from the General Preface that Alexander Campbell wrote for his emended edition of Campbell, MacKnight, and Doddridge's translation of the New Testament, first published at the end of January, 1826. (From *The Sacred Writings of the Apostles and Evangelists Commonly Styled the New Testament*, Bethany, Brooke Co., Va.: A. Campbell, 1826, pp. iii-xi).

An Apology for a New Translation

A living language is continually changing. Like the fashions and customs in apparel, words and phrases, at one time current and fashionable, in the lapse of time become awkward and obsolete. But this is not all; many of them, in a century or two, come to have a signification very different from that which was once attached to them: nay, some are known to convey ideas not only different from, but contrary to, their first signification. And were it not for books and parchments, which preserve from one generation to another, the language of the dead; and transmit from father to son, the words and sentences of past times; it is not improbable that, in one generation, a living language would undergo as many mutations, and admit of as many innovations, as it now does in two or three hundred years. Books, written in a style that obtains the reputation of being correct and elegant, serve to give stability to language. They are to language, what strongholds and fortresses are to a country. Yet even these the cankering hand of time molders away, and they cease to be a defense against invasion and revolution. And books, however reputable as the standard of a living tongue, and however much read and admired, are unable to maintain a long controversy against the versatility and love of novelty, characteristic of the human mind.

· · · · · · · · · · ·

But this constant mutation in a living language, will probably render new translations, or corrections of old translations, necessary every two or three hundred years. For although the English tongue may have changed less during the last two hundred years, than it ever did in the same lapse of time before: yet the changes which have taken place since the reign of James I, do now render a new translation necessary. For, if the King's translators had given a translation every way faithful and correct, in the language then spoken in Britain; the changes in the English language which have since been introduced, would render that translation, in many instances, incorrect.

· · · · · · · · · · ·

But in the preceding remarks it has been taken for granted, that the common version was an exact representation of the meaning of the original, at the time in which it was made. This, however, is not admitted by any sect in Christendom. All parties are occasionally finding fault. None are willing to abide by it in every sentence. It is, however, true, that the common version was made at a time when religious controversy was at its zenith; and that the tenets of the translators, whether designedly or undesignedly, did, on many occasions, give a wrong turn to words and sentences bearing upon their favorite dogmas.

52

It is much more likely, that we shall find a faithful and perspicuous translation coming from individuals who, without concert, or the solicitations of a party, undertake, and accomplish it, having no national or sectional cause to abet; than to expect to find one coming from those summoned by a King and his court, and paid for their services out of the public treasury: convened, too, from *one part* of those elements of discord which had distracted and convulsed a whole nation.

But another argument in favor of a new translation may be drawn from the fact, that we are now in possession of much better means of making an exact translation, than they were at the time when the common version appeared. The original is now much better understood than it was then. The conflicts of so many critics have elicited a great deal of sound critical knowledge, which was not in the possession of any translators before the last century. But as this topic has been so well handled, and so frequently argued by eminent writers, we shall not dwell on it.

To superficial readers many improvements in this version will appear of little importance; but to those who think more profoundly, some of the most minute alterations will throw a new light and luster on many passages. But of this every reader will judge after his own measure. We would only say, that the edification and comfort of Christians may be greatly promoted, by a minute examination of this version, and a diligent comparison of it with the common one.

If the mere publication of a version of the inspired writings requires, as we think it does, the publisher to have no sectarian object in view, we are happy in being able to appeal to our whole course of public addresses, and to all that we have written on religious subjects, to show that we have no such object in view. We have disclaimed and do again disclaim, all affection or partiality for any human system, creed, or formulary under heaven. The whole scope, design, and drift of our labor is, to see Christians intelligent, united, and happy. Believing that all sects have gone out of the apostolic way, and that every sect must go out of the way (for Christianity is in its nature hostile to each and to every sect), we will not, we can not, we dare not, do anything for the erection of a new one, or for assisting any now in existence in its human appendages. As to any predilection or preference to any one now existing, we have none, farther than they hold the traditions of the Apostles. As far as they hold fast these, we hold with them; and where they desert these, we desert them. . . . We oppose them most, who most oppose and depart from the simplicity, that is in Christ. I do most solemnly declare, that, as far as respects my feelings, partialities, reputation, and worldly interest as a man, I would become a Presbyterian, a Methodist, a Quaker, a Universalist, Socinian, or anything else, before the sun would set today, if the Apostolic writings would in my judgment authorize me in so doing; and that I would not give one turn to the meaning of an adverb, preposition, or interjectional, to aid any sectarian cause in the world. Whether every reader may give me credit in so declaring myself, I know not; but I thought it due to the occasion thus to express the genuine and unaffected feelings of my heart. May all, who honestly examine this version, abundantly partake of the blessings of that Spirit which guided the writers of this volume, and which in every page breathes, "Glory to God in the highest heaven, peace on earth, and good will among men."

1827

Campbell liked to keep his readers informed of his various travels. In early spring, 1827, he returned from a trip and wrote a lengthy description of his impressions for his readers. It was on a similar trip in 1824 that he first met Barton W. Stone and became acquainted with the Christian movement. (From *The Christian Baptist*, Vol. IV, No. 9, April 2, 1827, pp. 62-64).

Remarks on a Tour

Through the watchful care and supporting hand of the Father of Mercies, we have returned in safety from a tour in the states of Ohio, Kentucky, Indiana, and Tennessee, occupying a period of four months. On this tour I had the pleasure not only of visiting my old friends and acquaintances, but of adding many new ones to the number. To this pleasure, however, was annexed the pain of parting.

••••••••••

We added much to our knowledge of men and things religious, and returned home richly laden with materials for public edification. These materials have been quarried out of the actual condition of things in the religious world, and will require but little skill to adjust to advantage. . . . I would not raise expectations too high, . . . but I would say that I think I am better qualified to speak to the religious world on the subjects to which I have been calling attention than before. I have been questioned and cross-questioned a thousand times on a thousand topics; I have heard religious experiences, religious doubts; histories of conversions and relapses; of family religion, of family discipline, of Christian congregations, of councils, conferences, and synods, of debates and strifes, of revivals and declensions, of persecutions and triumphs, of religious wars and commotions—so numerous and diversified, so ordinary and extraordinary, that I think little can be added to give variety to the religious scenery which I now have in retrospect.

•••••••••••

Of the teachers of what is called religion, we have had a very full example. From the allegorizer, who preaches Christ and his church out of every verse of the Song of Solomon; from the mystic, who finds the whole plan of salvation in Paul's shipwreck and escape on Malta; from the inspired enthusiast, who tells of dreams and visions, of extacies and revelations all the day; from the drivelling paraphrast to the verbose and soporiferous commentator, we have had a perfect example. But on the other hand, we have also been conversant with the sapient doctors of biblical criticism, the shrewd and convincing reasoners upon the law and the testimony; the profound interpreters of scholastic theology; the eloquent declaimers against vice and immorality; the dispassionate and frigid metaphysician; the practical preacher, and the erudite bishop.

•••••••••••

The most generally true and correct report of the Baptist churches which could be given is as follows: — Four congregations or churches are under the pastoral care of one shepherd. He visits them every fourth Saturday and Sunday. In their church capacity they meet once a month. They meet at twelve on Saturday, and after organizing themselves by prayer and the appointment of a moderator for the day, business is called up. If there be no "business" on the docket an effort is made to create some, lest they should be idle. The business generally consists in hearing the experiences of candidates for baptism, should any offer. Each member becomes a juror, and when the candidate tells his story, a verdict is agreed on according to the nature of the case. If a favorable opinion of the candidate is entertained, he is ordered to be baptized; and this matter disposed of, nothing remains but to hear a sermon, or to quote the eighteenth of Matthew over some case of discipline.

The *first* day of the week, commonly called *Sunday*, is occupied in singing a few stanzas of something called hymns, which in general are the metrified articles of the creed of the church. Next comes a prayer, or the hymn turned into prose; that is, the opinions of the brethren, dressed up in the form of prayer; and then comes a sermon, in which one drop of wine is turned into a gallon of water. . . . And after being thus fed and feasted, the brethren go home for one month to ruminate and digest this hearty meal.

• • • • • • • • • •

This is not too highly colored for the present order of things on a general view; but we rejoice to know that there are many individual and some congregational exceptions.

• • • • • • • • • •

These remarks proceed from benevolence, and are designed not to flatter the wayward—not to allure the unsuspicious—not to conceal our shame—not to reproach the upright—not to palliate the froward—not to countenance the latitudinarians, nor to compliment the orthodox; but to warn, admonish, to reprove, confute and commend, when it is due. It is not he that commends himself who is approved, but him the Lord commends.

Editor

1827

The following short selection from *The Christian Baptist* is an indication of Campbell's growing sensitivity on the question of his "always being *against* something." Campbell is moving towards a more positive approach. (From *The Christian Baptist*, Vol. IV, No. 12, July 2, 1827, p. 14).

Potent Reply to a Weak Objection

"Pulling down every thing, and building up nothing," is an objection often presented against *The Christian Baptist*. The following reply to it from an English paper, is a perfect expression of our sentiments on the subject. The same things have in substance appeared in this work before.

Editor—*Christian Baptist*

"But the charge of pulling down and not building up any thing in its stead, is, unintentionally, the highest compliment that can be paid to us . . . .

"We have nothing to build up. The fair fabric of Christianity stands still as firm and conspicuous in the New Testament as ever it did; all we have got to do is to remove the walls, the buttresses and rubbish, which prevent inquiring men from beholding it in its native purity, splendor, and loveliness; and when this is done, the superstructure will present itself to view—an object deserving of universal admiration; then nothing more will be requisite than to invite men to examine it, as it is fairly and clearly depicted in the New Testament."

1829

After completing six volumes of *The Christian Baptist* and being aware of the increasing separation of the Disciples from the Baptists, Campbell determined to close that publication and to begin a new one; a periodical couched in more positive terms. The selection below contains Campbell's "Concluding Remarks" in the final issue of the journal. The first issues of *The Millennial Harbinger* already had appeared. (From *The Christian Baptist*, Vol. VII, No. 12, July 5, 1830, pp. 96-97)

Concluding Remarks
Part of the Editor's History

To the co-operation of a few friends, under the divine government, is to be ascribed the success which has accompanied this first effort to restore a pure speech to the people of God—to restore the ancient order of things in the Christian kingdom—to emancipate the conscience from the dominion of human authority in matters of religion, and to lay a foundation, an imperishable foundation, for the union of all Christians, and for their co-operation in spreading the glorious gospel throughout the world. I had but very humble hopes, I can assure the public, the day I wrote the first essay or the preface for this work, that I could at all succeed in gaining a patient hearing. . . .

Having been educated as Presbyterian clergymen generally are, and looking forward to the ministry as both an honorable and useful calling, all my expectations and prospects in future life were, at the age of twenty-one, identified with the office of the ministry. But scarcely had I begun to make sermons, when I discovered that the religion of the New Testament was one thing, and that of any sect which I knew was another. I could not proceed. An unsuccessful effort by my father to reform the presbytery and synod to which he belonged, made me despair of reformation. I gave it up as a hopeless effort: but did not give up speaking in public assemblies upon the great articles of Christian faith and practice. In the hope, the humble hope, of erecting a single congregation with which I could enjoy the social institutions, I labored. I had not the remotest idea of being able to do more than this; and, therefore, I betook myself to the occupation of a farmer, and for a number of years attended to this profession as a means of subsistence, and labored every Lord's day to separate the truth from the traditions of men, and to persuade men to give up their fables for the truth—with but little success I labored.

•••••••••••

In the year 1820, when solicited to meet Mr. Walker on the subject of baptism, I hesitated for about six months whether it were lawful thus to defend the truth. I was written to three times before I gained my own consent. I did not like controversy so well as many have since thought I did; and I was doubtful of the effects it might have upon society. These difficulties were, however, overcome, and we met. It was not until after I discovered the effects of that discussion that I began to hope that something might be done to rouse this generation from its supineness and spiritual lethargy. About two years afterwards I conceived the plan for this work. I did so, and the effects are now before the public.

•••••••••••

Many apologies ought to be made for the execution of the prospectus of this work. Things changed so much from our expectations that we were compelled to change with them. Our series of essays upon more topics were much shorter, and longer between, than was contemplated. The publication of two debates, and of two editions of the New Testament, unexpected when we issued our proposals, distracted our attentions, and so increased my labors, that more was done than could be done well.

•••••••••••

I have commenced a new work, and taken a new name for it on various accounts. Hating sects and sectarian names, I resolved to prevent the name of Christian Baptists from being fixed upon us, to which efforts were making. It is true, men's tongues are their own, and they may use them as they please; but I am resolved to give them no just occasion for nicknaming advocates for the ancient order of things. My sheet admonishes me that I must close, and as usual on such occasions, I ought to return thanks to all those who have aided in the circulation of this work and patronized it. . . . I have found myself blessed in this undertaking—my heart has been enlarged, and no reader of *The Christian Baptist*, I think will ever derive more advantage from it, than I have from the writing and conducting of it. To Jesus Christ my Lord be everlasting praise.

Editor

1830

On Monday, July 5, 1830, more than 120 members of the Church of Christ at Pittsburgh gathered in a grove about two miles from the city to hear an oration by Alexander Campbell in honor of the nation's civil government. In this address Campbell contrasts the freedom in Christ with civil freedom and the need to make oneself truly free by cultivating the things of the Spirit. (From *Popular Lectures and Addresses*, pp. 367-378).

A Fourth of July Oration

The cardinal principle in his government is love. He subdues by no other sword than that of the Spirit. Other kings subdue men's persons and hold a sovereignty over their estates, but he seizes the hearts of men. To conquer enemies is his grand enterprise. Philosophy as well as religion teaches us that to conquer enemies is not the work of swords, or lances, or bows of steel. It is not to bind many persons to a triumphal car, to incarcerate them in strongholds, or to make them surrender to superior bravery, prowess and strength. *To conquer an enemy is to convert him into a friend.* This is the noble, benevolent and heaven-conceived enterprise of God's only-begotten Son. To do this all arms and modes of warfare are impotent, save the arms and munitions of everlasting love. By vivid displays of God's philanthropy he approaches his enemies, and by arguments with which this eloquence is fraught he addresses a rebel world. Such is his mode of warfare; a system devised in heaven, and, like all of God's means, perfectly adapted to the high ends proposed.

•••••••••••

The *fourth of July*, 1776, was a memorable day, a day to be remembered as was the Jewish Passover—a day to be regarded with grateful acknowledgments by every American citizen, by every philanthropist in all the nations of the world. The light which shines from our political institutions will penetrate even the dungeons of European despots, *for the genius of our Government is the genius of universal emancipation!* Nothing can resist the political influence of a great nation, enjoying great political advantages, if she walk worthy of them.

•••••••••••

A more glorious work is reserved for this generation— a work of as much greater moment, compared with the Revolution of '76, as immortality is to the present span of human life—the emancipation of the human mind from the shackles of superstition, and the introduction of human beings into the full fruition of the reign of heaven. To liberate the minds of men from sectarian tyrannies— to deliver them from the melancholy thralldom of relentless systems, is a work fraught with greater blessings, a work of a nobler daring and loftier enterprise, than the substitution of the representative democracy for an absolute or limited monarchy. This revolution, taken in all its influences, will make men free indeed. A political revolution can only make men politically free to task themselves, and to exact from themselves a service which few of the despots of more barbarous climes inflict upon their veriest slaves.

Talk not of liberty which only makes men greater slaves. Under the monarchies of the Old World men are more free from themselves than under the free government of these United States. The reason is, under this free government the citizens have the opportunity and the liberty of improving and bettering their circumstances to such an extent as to engross all their energies, to call forth all their powers: hence, upon themselves they impose such tasks and inflict such toils and privations as few of the monarchies of the East would be so cruel as to impose upon their subjects. Here in this land of liberty we see all men striving for power. The accomplishment of one or more projects does not diminish their labor or their enterprise. Quite the reverse: the more successful, the more eager to commence again. And how often, how very often, do we see men dying under the whip of their own cupidity, in full harness pulling up the hill of their own ambition, when death kindly interposes, takes the burden off their galled shoulders, and strips them for the shroud! Yet they boast of being free! Free!—yes,to make slaves of themselves! If the Son of God had made them free, they would not thus toil till the last pulsation of their hearts.

●●●●●●●●●●

Conscience makes slaves as well as cowards of multitudes who boast of being free. No person who is under the fear of death ever can be free. They who are afraid of the consequences of death are all their lifetime in bondage. To escape from this vassalage is worthy of the greatest struggle which man could make. This, however, is the first boon which Christianity tenders to all who put themselves under its influence. It proclaims a jubilee to the soul—it opens the prison-doors, and sets the captive free. The corruptions of anti-Christian systems are admirably adapted to increase and cherish this fear, which tends to bondage; but to those who embrace and bow to the real gospel, there is bestowed a full deliverance, and a gracious exemption from this most grievous bondage of the soul.

1836

The following selection is taken from an address on the importance of teaching that Campbell delivered to the College of Teachers, Cincinnati, Ohio in October, 1836. Bishop John B. Purcell of the Roman Catholic Church was in his audience and took exception to some of his statements. It was this address that occasioned Campbell's debate with Bishop Purcell. (From *Popular Lectures and Addresses*, pp. 481-483).

On Teaching and Morals

Permit one who for several years has experienced your toils, who has felt your responsibilities and shared in the pleasure of your calling, both in Europe and America, to remind you that you are engaged in an object of superlative importance, not only to the present generation, but that, in a good measure, is intrusted to you the destiny of the future. The youth of this generation are the hope of the next; and, consequently, in forming the intellectual and moral character of this germ of future generations, you cannot but in some good degree shape their destiny. But, further than this, gentlemen, your influence extends beyond the mere temporal conditions of our being. On the bias which you may give in favor of truth and moral principle, may depend the eternal destiny of many generations. Next to the parents of your pupils, you possess a power over human character paramount to any officers in the whole community—I would say, if I had time to qualify it, beyond even the ministers of religion. It is only sometimes that we can trace to the conscientiousness and benevolence of an individual benefactor the happiness and prosperity of a whole community; . . . And, were we more observant of the concatenation of things in the way of cause and effect, we would more frequently find that to the nursery and to the school we are indebted for that first impulse which has turned the current of human action into a new channel and materially changed the complexion of society for many generations. May it not, then, be in your power—co-operating, as you do, in your efforts to introduce a more philosophical and moral system of education in harmony with the human constitution—to stamp a character upon future times alike honorable to yourselves and beneficial to the world?

Give me leave, gentlemen, to say to you, and, through you, to all intrusted with the formation of a better character, for the next and future generations, than that which the present has attained, that this cause can never flourish as it ought till the public mind is so imbued with its importance and practicability as to make it the paramount duty of the whole government of every State to take into its most grave and deliberate consideration the whole chapter of the ways and means by which it will be impossible for ignorant and vicious parents to exist, or, if existing, to corrupt their offspring; and by which a solid, substantial, literary and moral education shall be made accessible to every child born upon its territory, and not only accessible, but unavoidable in all cases where nature has not withheld the powers and susceptibilities necessary to its attainment.

It is only, indeed, when the maxim that intelligence and virtue are the essential pillars of the state shall have deeply penetrated the public mind and indelibly engraven itself upon the apprehension of all, that it will become entirely obvious that it is incomparably more rational and commendable to legislate for the training of children

66

than for the punishment of vicious men; that it is much more economical and philanthropic to raise funds to educate and discipline youth in the paths of true science and moral excellence than to erect houses of correction or to provide ways and means of preventing rapine, violence and murder, or of suppressing tumults and insurrections among the people; that the rational education of youth is the highest object to the whole community—to the patriot, the philanthropist and the Christian; and that those who will improve and elevate its character and facilitate its operations are to be honored and ranked amongst the most useful citizens and the best benefactors of mankind.

You have the honor, gentlemen, of having begun at the right place, of having selected the best subject in existence on which to concentrate your powers of doing good. While other friends of human kind—the patriot, the politician and the economist—have taken the country— its convenience, its trade, its commerce, its resources— under their kind auspices, you have wisely selected the human species—the human soul itself—on which to exercise all your powers of doing good. If, then, he who, by his science and devotion to his country's interest, has made two blades of grass grow where formerly nature produced but one, is worthy to be ranked amongst a nation's benefactors, how large the dimensions of his fame, how wide the circumference of that Christian's glory, who shall have doubled, trebled, and perhaps more than quadrupled, the powers and capacities of his race for knowing, for doing and for enjoying good!

1838

The selection which follows is taken from a larger address entitled "Address on Literature, Science and Art" given in 1838 to the students at New Athens College (now University of Ohio). This was some ten to twelve years before the publication of Darwin's *Origin of Species* but anticipates some of the questions that book was to raise and insists on keeping a unity between these two aspects of truth. (From *Popular Addresses and Lectures*, pp. 136-141).

On Science and Religion

There remains but one point to consummate our plan—the connection of science, all true science, with religion. One might as rationally seek to comprehend an effect without any knowledge of its cause, as to comprehend any part of the science of the universe without some knowledge of its Author. God and his works are the basis of all the science in the world. But as the universe is not without God, nor God not without his universe, so no science, physical or ethical, can be thoroughly learned without the revealed knowledge of God. We study man in his works and in his word, and we contemplate our Creator through the medium of what he has done and said.

The works of God are his first and most ancient revelation of himself; and had not man, by his apostasy, lost the art of reading and studying the works of God, he would not have stood in need of any other medium of knowing him, or of communicating with him, than this wonderful and greatly diversified volume of nature. And, even as it is, the intelligent Christian makes the greatest proficiency in studying nature and the Bible by making them subservient to each other—sometimes interpreting the Bible by nature, and at other times expounding nature by the Bible. They are two voices speaking for God—two witnesses of his being and perfections; but neither of them is wholly adequate to meet all the variety of human circumstance without the other.

But we need no more striking evidence of the intimate connection between science and the Bible than the well-established fact, that all the great masters of science were believers in the Bible and cherished the hopes which it inspires. Bacon, the founder of the inductive philosophy; Locke, the great mental and moral philosopher; and Newton, the interpreter and revealer of nature's secrets, are known to the religious as well as to the scientific world as believers in the Bible and expounders of its doctrine, its precepts, types and promises. They are as eminent for their homage to the Bible as for their devotion to the studies of nature. Philosophy, with them, and Christianity were not at variance.

They saw the immutable and inimitable traces and characters of one and the same Supreme Intelligence clearly and boldly written on every page of the volumes of Creation, Providence and Redemption. They were persuaded that the still small voice which whispers in every star and in every flower speaks aloud in the language of authority and of love in all the precepts and promises of the law and of the gospel. Such were the great founders of the reigning philosophy and sciences of the present day. But I speak not of the first class only; for it seems as if the Father of Lights had vouchsafed all useful sciences, discoveries and arts to those who acknowledged his being and perfections, and to none else. So general if not universal, is this feature of his providence, that I know not the name of the founder of any science, or the inventor of any useful art, or the discoverer of any great master-truth in any department of human thought, who did not acknowledge the God of the Bible and cherish the hope of a future life.

69

••••••••••

It was observed that one of the principal difficulties in the proper classification of science and of human knowledge is found in the fact that all the sciences run into each other, and are separated rather by gradations than by clear and prominent lines of demarcation. Now, if this be true in physics and ethics, it is most certainly and evidently true of their connection and intimacy with religion. In the natural sciences we cannot advance a single step without the perception of adaptation and design.... Thus the whole solar system seems to exist for our earth; our earth for its vegetable and animal productions; and these, again, for man. Our earth, however, appears to be adapted to the universe as the universe is to it.... Thus the whole universe, both in its general laws and in its particular arrangements, is one immense system of means and ends, suggesting to the true philosopher one great First Cause and one grand Last End, between which all things exist.

••••••••••

To me it has ever been a paradox, a mystery, how any one can feast on nature, or luxuriate in the high enjoyment of the arcana which science reveals—how any one can in ecstasy and rapture contemplate the celestial and the terrestrial wonders of creation, and yet be indifferent either to the character or will of Him who is himself infinitely more wonderful and glorious than they—how any one can admire the developments of the Creator, and forbear himself to adore. Assuredly there is something wrong, some superlative inconsistency or mistake in this matter; else it would be impossible to delight in the work and neglect or despise the workman.

When education shall be adapted to the human constitution and conducted in full reference to the rank and dignity of man, then will the connection of science and religion, of nature and God, be made not merely the subject of an occasional lecture, but a constant study; the universe will then be but a comment on the Supreme

Intelligence; the being, perfections, providence and will of the Almighty Father will always be the text; and every science but a practical view of Him in whom we live and are moved and have our being, and of our responsibilities and obligations to Him who has endowed us with these noble faculties and powers, on account of which we rejoice and triumph in existence.

Meanwhile . . . I would remind you that there is one science, and one art springing from it, which is the chief of all the sciences and of all the arts taught in all the schools under these broad heavens. That science, as defined by the Great Teacher, is the knowledge of God and of Jesus Christ whom he has commissioned. This, he says, is eternal life. And that are which springs from it is the noblest and finest in the universe: it is the art of doing justly, of loving mercy, and of walking humbly with our God.

1839

In two editorials in consecutive issues of *The Millennial Harbinger*, Campbell dealt with the question of name: Disciples—Christians—Reformers—Campbellites? The question of name had been discussed previously as early as 1830 with Barton W. Stone and others. As many persons today can testify the question is still with us. (From *The Millennial Harbinger*, Vol. III, No. VIII, August, l839, pp. 337-339 and Vol. III, No. IX, September, 1839, pp. 401-403).

Our Name
First Editorial—August, 1839

What shall we be called? is one question; and *What shall men call us*? is another. We are responsible for the first—our neighbors for the second. There is virtue, or there is vice—moral good, or moral evil on both sides. If we miscall ourselves, the sin is ours—it is theirs, if they do it.

We all agree that there is potency in a name. The world is ruled by names, both in a good and in a bad sense. If this be true, we exert an influence, good or evil, by the name we wear, as we do by the character we form. It is of importance, then, that *we be called* what we are, as that *we be* what we are called.

72

The Lutherans, Calvinists, Arminians, judging us according to their standard, and weighing us in their balances, have nicknamed us *"Campbellites."* They wish us to take no precedence of them. They are proud of the livery they wear, and would have us to be like themselves—the followers of a fallible earthly leader. But our Master forbids us to assume any such designation, as derogatory to him, to ourselves, and tending to schism.

Some would have us call ourselves *Reformers*, as if this word was specific of any thing. Like the word *Protestant*, it means nothing positive or definite, either in principle or in practice.

Some like the name *"Bible Christians,"* as if there were Christians without the Bible. . . .

I am a Baptist, a Presbyterian, an Episcopalian, a Congregationalist, a Methodist, a Catholic, in the proper unappropriated sense of these words. But not one of them, nor all of them, express my views, my profession, or my practice as a disciple of Christ. In other words, I am an immerser; I believe in a presbytery or eldership in every congregation, and in overseers of the flock. I regard every community as independent of every other in what concerns its own internal acts and regulations—I am *methodical* in my arrangements and proceedings—and *Catholic* in all my charities, as I am in the doctrine, morality, and piety of the gospel. But all of these terms do not fully nor perfectly represent my religious profession; therefore I would falsify if I chose any one of them, or all of them, as representative of my profession as a religious man.

We have, then, only to choose between two scriptural titles—*"Disciples"* and *"Christians."* Of their respective claims upon our attention, next month.

Second Editorial—September, 1839

Into what, or into whom have we been immersed? Into Calvin, Luther, Wesley, Campbell, or Reformation? If not, then why nickname us, or we nickname ourselves,

73

when we assume or choose such designations? Shall we be called Disciples of Christ, or Christians? Why not call ourselves Christians? Not because we have another leader than Christ; for he is our teacher. We believe in him—were immersed into his death—and have thus put on Christ. But we have been anticipated. The term *Christian* in New England, and in some other sections of this land, is a name chosen and appropriated by a party who boast that they are *Unitarians*—disbelieve in baptism for the remission of sins—and refuse to celebrate the Lord's death as often as they celebrate his resurrection, etc. . . .

For this reason we prefer an unappropriated name, which is indeed neither more nor less than the scriptural equivalent of *Christian*; for who were called Christians first at Antioch? They had a prior—a more ancient name. They were called *Disciples*. Disciples of whom? Of Christ. *Disciples of Christ* is, then, a more ancient title than *Christian*, while it fully includes the whole idea. It is, then, as divine, as authoritative as the name *Christian*, and more ancient. Besides, it is more descriptive; and, better still, it is unappropriated. It claims our preference for four reasons:

        1st. It is more ancient.
        2nd. It is more descriptive.
        3rd. It is more scriptural.
        4th. It is more unappropriated.

1. Our first reason is indisputable; for the *disciples of Christ* were called Christians *first in Antioch*. Those who from the day of Pentecost were known throughout Judea, Galilee, Samaria, and among the Gentiles as disciples of Christ, were, at Antioch, many years afterwards, called, for the first time, *Christians*.

2. It is more *descriptive*: because many people are named after their country, or their political leaders, and sometimes after their religious leaders, who would feel it an insult to be called the pupils or disciples of the person whose name they bear. . . .

3. It is more *scriptural*. Luke wrote his Acts some thirty years after the ascension. Now in his writings, which give at least thirty years' history of the primitive church, the word *Christian* occurs but twice—used only by the *Antiochans* and by king Agrippa; *but no disciple, as far as Luke relates, ever spoke of himself or brethren under that designation. More than thirty times they are called Disciples* in the Acts of the Apostles. Luke and other intelligent men call them often *"brethren"* and *"disciples,"* but never Christians. . . .

4. It is more unappropriated at the present time. Unitarians, Arians, and sundry other newly risen sects abroad, are zealous for the name *Christian*; while we are the only people on earth fairly and indisputably in the use of the title *Disciples of Christ*.

For these four reasons I prefer this designation to any other which has been offered. Can any one offer better reasons for a better name?

A.C.

1839

Of all Campbell's writings no one of them probably had more influence than *The Christian System, in Reference to the Union of Christians and a Restoration of Primitive Christianity, as Plead in the Current Reformation* (Bethany, Va.: printed by A. Campbell, 1839); in fact, it is still in print. An earlier version was published in 1835 under the title *A Connected View of the Principles and Rules by Which the Living Oracles May Be Intelligibly and Certainly Interpreted* (Bethany, Va.: M'Vay and Ewing, 1835). Selections have been taken from the Preface to the First Edition, the Preface to the Second Edition and from several sections of the book.

The Christian System
(From the Preface to the First Edition)

We Americans owe our national privileges and our civil liberties to the Protestant Reformers. They achieved not only an imperishable fame for themselves, but a rich legacy for their posterity. When we contrast the present state of these United States with Spanish America, and the condition of the English nation with that of Spain, Portugal, and Italy, we begin to appreciate how much we are indebted to the intelligence, faith and courage of Martin Luther and his heroic associates in that glorious reformation.

He restored the Bible to the world in A.D. 1534, and boldly defended its claims against the impious and arrogant pretensions of the haughty and tyrannical See of Rome. But, unfortunately, at his death there was no Joshua to lead the people, who rallied under the banners of the Bible, out of the wilderness in which Luther died. His tenets were soon converted into a new state religion, and the spirit of the Reformation which he excited and inspirited was soon quenched by the broils and feuds of the Protestant princes, and the collisions of rival political interests, both on the continent and in the islands of Europe.

•••••••••••

Since that time, the first effort known to us to abandon the whole controversy about creeds and reformations, and to *restore* primitive Christianity, or to build alone upon the Apostles and Prophets, Jesus Christ himself the chief corner, has been made.

Tired of new creeds and new parties in religion, and of the numerous abortive efforts to reform the reformation; convinced from the Holy Scriptures, from observation and experience, that the union of the disciples of Christ is essential to the conversion of the world, and that the correction and improvement of no creed, or partisan establishment in Christendom, could ever become the basis of such a union, communion and co-operation, as would restore peace to a church militant against itself, or triumph to the common salvation; a few individuals, about the commencement of the present century, began to reflect upon the ways and means to restore primitive Christianity.

The Bible alone is the Bible only, in word and deed, in profession and practice; and this alone can reform the world and save the church. Judging others as we once judged ourselves, there are not a few who are advocating the Bible alone, and preaching their own opinions. Before we applied the Bible alone to our views, or brought our views and religious practices to the Bible, we plead the old theme, "The Bible alone is the religion of Protestants." But we found it an arduous task, and one of twenty years' labor, to correct our diction and purify our speech according to the Bible alone; and even yet we have not wholly practically repudiated the language of Ashdod. . . .

A deep and an abiding impression that the power, the consolations and joys—the holiness and happiness—of Christ's religion were lost in the forms and ceremonies, in the speculations and conjectures, in the feuds and bickerings of sects and schisms, originated a project many years ago for uniting the sects, or rather the *Christians* in all the sects, upon a clear and scriptural bond of union,— upon having a *"thus saith the Lord,"* either in express terms or in approved precedent, "for every article of faith, and item of religious practice." This was offered in the year 1809, in the "Declaration and Address" of the Washington Association, Pennsylvania. It was first tendered to the parties that confessed the Westminster creed; but equally submitted to the Protestants of every name, making faith in Christ and obedience to him the only *test* of Christian character, and the only *bond* of church union, communion, and co-operation. It was indeed approved by all; but adopted and practiced by none, except the few, or part of the few, who made the future.

(From the Preface to the Second Edition)

We speak for ourselves only; and, while we are always willing to give a declaration of our faith and knowledge of the Christian system, we firmly protest against dogmatically propounding our own views, or those of any fallible mortal, as a condition or foundation of church union and co-operation. While, then, we would, if we could, either with the tongue or the pen, proclaim all that we believe, and all that we know, to the ends of the earth, *we take the Bible, the whole Bible, and nothing but the Bible as the foundation of all Christian union and communion.* Those who do not like this will please show us a more excellent way.

The Bible (Chapter II)

I. One God, one moral system, one Bible. If nature be a system, religion is no less so. God is "a God of order," and that is the same as to say he is a God of system. Nature and religion, the offspring of the same supreme intelligence, bear the image of one father—twin-sisters of the same divine parentage. This is an intellectual and a moral universe as clearly bounded as the system of material nature. Man belongs to the whole three. He is an animal, intellectual, and moral being. *Sense* is his guide in nature, *faith* in religion, *reason* in both. The Bible contemplates man primarily in his spiritual and eternal relation. It is the history of nature so far only as is necessary to show man his origin and destiny, for it contemplates nature—the universe—only in relation to man's body, soul, and spirit.

II. The Bible is to the intellectual and moral world of man what the sun is to the planets in our system,—the fountain and source of light and life, spiritual and eternal. There is not a spiritual idea in the whole human race that is not drawn from the Bible. As soon will the philosopher find an independent sunbeam in nature, as the theologian spiritual conception in man, independent of The One Best Book.

III. The Bible, or the Old and New Testaments, in Hebrew and Greek, contains a full and perfect revelation of God and his will, adapted to man as he now is. It speaks of man as he was, and also as he will hereafter be: but it dwells on man *as he is*, and *as he ought to be*, as its peculiar and appropriate theme. It is not, then, a treatise on man as he was, nor on man as he will be; but on man as he is, and as he ought to be; not as he is physically, astronomically, geologically, politically, or metaphysically; but as he is and ought to be, *morally* and *religiously*.

IV. The words of the Bible contain all the ideas in it. These words, then, rightly understood, and the ideas are clearly perceived. The words and sentences of the Bible are to be translated, interpreted, and understood according to the same code of laws and principles of interpretation by which other ancient writings are translated and understood; for, when God spoke to man in his own language, he spoke as one person converses with another,—in the fair, stipulated, and well-established meaning of the terms. This is essential to its character as a revelation from God; otherwise it would be no revelation, but would always require a class of inspired men to unfold and reveal its true sense to mankind.

V. We have written frequently and largely upon the principle and rules of interpretation, as of essential importance and utility in this generation of remaining mysticizing and allegorizing. From our former writings we shall here only extract the naked rules of interpretation, deduced from extensive and well-digested premises; fully sustained, too, by the leading translators and most distinguished critics and commentators of the last and present century.

VI. Rule 1. On opening any book in the sacred Scriptures, *consider first the historical circumstances of the book. These are the order, the title, the author, the date, the place, and the occasion of it.*

The *order* in historical compositions is of much importance; as, for instance, whether the first, second, or third, of the five books of Moses, or of any other series of narrative, or even epistolatory communications.

The *title* is also of importance, as it sometimes expresses the *design* of the book. As *Exodus*—the departure of Israel from Egypt, *Acts of Apostles*, etc.

The peculiarities of the *author*, the age in which he lived, his style, mode of expression, illustrate his writings. The date, place, and occasion of it, are obviously necessary to a right application of any thing in the book.

Rule 2. In examining the contents of any book, as respects precepts, promises, exhortations, etc.; *observe who it is that speaks, and under what dispensation he officiates.* Is he a Patriarch, a Jew, or a Christian? *Consider also the persons addressed, their prejudices, characters and religious relations.* Are they Jews or Christians, believers or unbelievers, approved or disapproved? This rule is essential to the proper application of every command, promise, threatening, admonition, or exhortation, in Old Testament or New.

Rule 3. To understand the meaning of what is commanded, promised, taught, etc., *the same philological principles deduced from the nature of language, or the same laws of interpretation which are applied to the language of other books, are to be applied to the language of the Bible.*

Rule 4. *Common usage, which can only be ascertained by testimony, must always decide the meaning of any word which has but one signification*; but when words have, according to the testimony, (i.e., the Dictionary) more meanings than one, whether literal or figurative, *the scope, the context, or parallel passages must decide the meaning*: for if common usage, the design of the writer, the context, and parallel passages fail, there can be no certainty in the interpretation of language.

Rule 5. *In all tropical language ascertain the point of resemblance, and judge of the nature of the trope, and its kind, from the point of resemblance.*

Rule 6. In the interpretation of symbols, types, allegories and parables, this rule is supreme: —*Ascertain the point to be illustrated; for comparison is never to be extended beyond that point to all the attributes, qualities, or circumstances of the symbol, type, allegory, or parable.*

Rule 7. For the salutary and sanctifying intelligence of the Oracles of God, the following rule is indispensable: —*We must come within the understanding distance.*

There is a distance which is properly called the *speaking distance*, or *the hearing distance*; beyond which the voice reaches not, and the ear hears not. To hear another, we must come within that circle which the voice audibly fills.

Now we may with propriety say, that as it respects God, there is an understanding distance. All beyond that distance cannot understand God; all within it can easily understand him in all matters of piety and morality. God himself is the centre of that circle, and humility is its circumference.

Baptism (Chapter XVI)

I. There are three things to be considered in baptism: 1. The action commanded to be done; 2. The subject specified; 3. The meaning or design of that action. Jesus commanded a certain *character* to be the subject of a certain *action*, for a certain specific purpose or *design*.

II. The action is indicated by a word as definite, clear, and unequivocal, as any word in any language ever spoken by the many-tongued sons of Adam.

III. That definite and unambiguous word, as almost universally known in these days of controversy, is *baptisma* or *baptismos*, anglicized, not translated, *baptism*. The ancient lexicons with one consent, give *immersion* as the natural, common, and primary sense of this word. All Latin, English, German and French versions which we have seen, and we believe on the testimony of others, all that we have not seen, sometimes translate these words, or their derivatives, or compounds, by words equivalent to *immersion*; but on *no occasion* ever translate them by sprinkling, or pouring, or any word equivalent to these terms. The ancient church, it is admitted on all hands, practiced immersion. It did so, Roman, Greek and English historians being worthy of any credit.

IV. *Characters*, not *persons*, as such, are the subjects of baptism. *Penitent believers*—not infants nor adults, not males nor females, not Jews or Greeks; but professors of repentance towards God, and faith in Christ—are the proper subjects of this ordinance.

V. Baptism is, then, designed to introduce the subjects of it into the participation of the blessings of the death and resurrection of Christ; who "died for our sins," and "rose again for our justification." . . . to the believing penitent it is the *means* of receiving a formal, distinct and specific absolution, or release from guilt. Therefore, none but those who have first believed the testimony of God and have repented of their sins, and that have been intelligently immersed into his death, have the full and explicit testimony of God, assuring them of pardon.

The Body of Christ (Chapter XXIV)

I. That institution which separates from the world, and consociates the people of God into a peculiar community; having laws, ordinances, manners and customs of its own, immediately derived from the Saviour of the world, is called the *congregation* or *church* of the Lord. This is sometimes technically called the *mystical* body of Christ, contradistinguished from his literal and natural body. Over this spiritual body he is the Head, the King, Lord and Lawgiver, and they are severally members of his body, and under his direction and government.

II. The *true* Christian church, or house of God, is composed of all those in every place that do publicly acknowledge Jesus of Nazareth as the true Messiah, and the only Saviour of men; and, building themselves upon the foundation of the Apostles and prophets, associate under the constitution which he himself has granted and authorized in the New Testament, and are walking in his ordinances and commandments—and none else.

III. This institution, called *the congregation of God*, is a great community of communities—not a community representative of communities, but a community composed of many particular communities, each of which is built upon the same foundation, walks according to the same rules, enjoys the same charter, and is under the jurisdiction of no other community of Christians, but is to all other communities as an individual disciple is to every other individual disciple in any one particular community meeting in any given place.

IV. Still, all these particular congregations of the Lord, whether at Rome, Corinth, or Ephesus, though equally independent of one another as to the management of their own peculiar affairs, are, by virtue of one common Lord, one faith, one baptism, and one common salvation, but one kingdom or church of God, and, as such, are under the obligations to co-operate with one another in all measures promotive of the great ends of Christ's death and resurrection.

V. But, in order to this holy communion and co-operation of churches, it is indispensable that they have an intimate and approving knowledge of one another, which can only be had and enjoyed in the form of districts. And while some of the churches or brethren in each district, being mutually acquainted with some in another, made the churches of both districts acquainted with one another, they were enabled to co-operate to the ends of the earth.

VI. These districts are a part of the *circumstances* of Christ's kingdom, as well as the *manner* of maintaining correspondence and co-operation among them, and the occasions and incidents requiring concert and conjoint action. For these, as well as for the circumstances of any particular community, the Apostles gave no specific directions.

VII. But in granting to the communities of the saints this necessary license of deciding what is expedient, orderly, decent, and of public and practical utility in the circumstantials of Christianity, no allowance is implied authorizing any interference with a single item of the Christian institution. Hence the necessity of a very clear discrimination, not between "the essentials and the non-essentials," for in Divine Christianity there are no non-essentials, but between the family of God and its circumstances, between the Christian institution and its accidents.

VIII. The Christian institution has its facts, its precepts, its promises, its ordinances, and their meaning or doctrine. These are not matters of policy, of arrangement, of expediency, but of divine and immutable ordination and continuance. Hence the faith, the worship, and the righteousness; or the doctrine, the piety, and the morality of the gospel institution are not legitimate subjects of human legislation, alteration, or arrangement.

IX. But whether we shall register the churches in a given district, or the members in a particular church; whether we shall meet oftener than once on the Lord's day, or at what hour, and in what sort of a house; whether we shall commemorate the Lord's death forenoon or afternoon, before day or after night; . . . whether we shall sing from book or from memory, prose or verse, etc. etc., are matters in which our conceptions of expediency, decency, and good order may have free scope. Also whether the churches in a given district shall, by letter, messengers, or stated meetings, once or twice per annum, or oftener, communicate with one another; whether they shall send one, two or twenty persons, or all go and communicate face to face, or send a letter; and whether they shall annually print, write, or publish their statistics, etc., are all the mere circumstantials of the Christian institution.

X. But co-operation itself is one thing, and the manner of co-operation is another. Co-operation, as much as the intercommunion of Christians, is a part of the Christian institution. We must *"strive together* in our prayers" for one another, and for the salvation of men; and this, if there were no scriptural example nor precept on the subject, is enough. To pray for one another as individuals or communities implies that we shall assist one another in every way for which we pray for one another; otherwise our prayers and thanksgivings for each other are mere hypocrisy. He that would pray for the progress of the truth at home and abroad, having it in his power to contribute a single dollar to that end, and yet withholds it, shows how little value he sets upon his own prayers, and how much upon his money.

XI. From the days of the Apostles till now co-operative associations of churches have uniformly followed the political distributions of the earth. This is a matter of convenience, rather than of necessity; just as the churches in Pennsylvania, Virginia, Ohio, Kentucky, etc. can generally more conveniently and successfully co-operate by states and territories, than by any other divisions or precincts. I say, this is a matter of convenience, rather than of necessity. It is of necessity that we co-operate, but of convenience that the churches in one county, state, or nation form regular ways and means for co-operation.

XII. The necessity of co-operation is felt everywhere and in all associations of men. It is a part of the economy of Heaven. One hundred churches, well disciplined, acting in concert, with Christian zeal, piety, humanity—frequently meeting together in committees of ways and means for building up Zion, for fencing in the deserts, cultivating the enclosed fields, watering the dry and barren spots, striving together mightily in prayer, in preaching the word, in contributing to the necessities of the saints, in enlightening the ignorant, and in devising all practicable ways of doing good—would, in a given period, do more than twice the same number acting in their individual capacity, without concert, without co-operation, and that united energy, always the effect of intelligent and cordial combination.

XIII. But, in order to this, Christians must regard the church, or body of Christ, as one community, though composed of many small communities, each of which is an organized member of this great national organization; which, under Christ, as the supreme and sole Head, King, Lord, and Lawgiver, has the conquest of the whole world in its prayers, aims, plans, and efforts. Hence there must be such an understanding and agreement between these particular congregations as will suffice to a recognition and approval of their several acts; so that the members or the measures of one community shall be treated with the respect due to them at home, in whatever community they may happen to be presented.

XIV. Any one who seeks apostolic sanctions for these views of co-operation will find ample authority in the Acts and Epistles of the Apostles. The very basis of such general or universal letters is the fact, that all the communities of Christ constitute but one body, and are individually and mutually bound to co-operate in all things pertaining to a common salvation.

1842

Questions were raised regarding whether cooperation between congregations was possible in a New
Testament church and what kind of church organization would be scriptural. Campbell's answer
came in a series of articles in *The Millennial Harbinger*. In the volume for 1842 there are no less
than eight long articles on "The Nature of Christian Organization" and a short article entitled
"Five Arguments for Church Organization," which
is printed below. (From *The Millennial Harbinger*,
Vol. VI, Number XI, November, 1842, p. 523).

On Co-operation

Great need of a more rational and scriptural organization

1. We can do comparatively but little in distributing
the Bible abroad without co-operation.

2. We can do comparatively but little in the great missionary field of the world either at home or abroad without co-operation.

3. We can do little or nothing to improve and elevate
the Christian ministry without co-operation.

4. We can do little to check, restrain, and remove the
flood of imposture and fraud committed upon the benevolence of the brethren by irresponsible, plausible, and
deceptious persons, without co-operation.

5. We cannot concentrate the action of the tens of
thousands of Israel, in any great Christian effort, but by
co-operation.

We can have no thorough co-operation without a more
ample, extensive, and thorough church organization.

These five points are enough for one lesson.

A.C.

1845

The question of slavery increasingly disturbed the Christian community. The year 1845 saw the separation of the Baptist and the Methodist churches into divisions of the North and the South. Campbell felt it necessary to give major attention to the subject for Disciples. No less than fourteen articles on slavery are to be found in *The Millennial Harbinger* for that year. The selections which follow are from the first and the tenth of these editorials. They give most forcefully Campbell's judgment at this stage of the controversy. (From *The Millennial Harbinger*, Third Series, Vol. II, No. 11, February, 1845, pp. 49-53 and Third Series, Vol. II, No. VI, June, 1845, pp. 257-264).

Our Position to American Slavery
Editorial—February, 1845

When any nation or people resolve to be free,—when they publicly renounce all allegiance, all political subordination to any foreign prince or potentate, they institute an example of doubtful and dangerous tendency. They cannot calculate upon its influence and bearings upon society in many other particulars besides that in their immediate vision. When, in solemn convention, the assembled representatives of a nation affirm before *High Heaven* that "all men are born free and equal," they promulgate views and resolves which are not to be circumscribed by the particular objects which on that particular occasion called them together. When a nation guarantees to every citizen "liberty of thought, liberty of speech, and liberty of action," with only a few constitutional restraints and limitations, it confers powers of doing good, which, in certain circumstances, may work its salvation; but it must also be confessed that, in other circumstances, it may confer powers of doing evil which may work its ruin. One thing is most evident, that without intelligence and virtue on the part of the people, such chartered rights are dangerous investments. Wise and patriotic men have, therefore, questioned the propriety of vouchsafing such ample liberties without providing for the intellectual and moral culture of the whole population. The right of suffrage, in every well regulated community, ought, in their opinion, always to have a *moral*, never a *property* qualification.

•••••••••••

Any one of much sagacity must see that the controversy between the North and the South has commenced. As certain, too, as that no one can live in Rome and strive against the Pope, must the whole Northern and Southern institutions come before the whole American family. Already, indeed, has it come into our American ecclesiastical courts, and distracted the councils of one of the most imposing communities in our Protestant ranks. Nor does this state of things appear to be exclusively conferred to any one of the Protestant sects of our country: other denominations, because of the politico-ecclesiastic character of their association, must be constrained to take the same ground.

We are the only religious community in the civilized world whose principles (unless we abandon them) can preserve us from such an unfortunate predicament. This I feel able to demonstrate to the entire satisfaction of every intelligent brother and candid citizen at the South or at the North. Lend me your ears and allow me a seasonable opportunity, and my facts and arguments shall be forthcoming.

The cardinal question affecting us, then, is—*What does the Bible teach on this subject?*—not what natural reason, natural conscience, or the opinions of men may dictate, or what human prudence and expediency may allow. . . .

A.C.

Editorial—June, 1845

By this time, it is presumed, that our position in relation to the institution of Slavery may be ascertained with general, if not with very particular, accuracy. Still, unwilling to leave anything to the hazard of unwarrantable to doubtful inference, we deem it proper to deduce our own conclusions and to state our position in terms the most clear and definite. This we shall attempt in the form of inferences or conclusions from premises already laid down, accompanied with some farther illustrations.

1st. From a full induction of the laws, statutes, and usages of the patriarchs, Jews, and Christians, as reported in the writings of Moses and of the Apostles, and sanctioned by numerous divine enactments and regulations, we conclude that *the relation of master and slave is no where condemned in the Holy Scriptures as morally wrong; and that, in certain cases, and under certain regulations, it is even now altogether lawful and right.*

If it should be any satisfaction to any of my readers, I will add, that, although for many years I have regarded the institution of American slavery as not in harmony with the spirit and genius of this age, nor with the peculiar genius of our American population and political institutions, and by my education strongly prejudiced against it, still, on every examination of the Sacred Scriptures on this subject for many years past, and these have been neither few nor long between, I have always been compelled to this conclusion.

While, then, I have most sincerely and conscientiously, for many years, held and expressed these opinions, I have been so much opposed to American slavery *because of its abuses and liabilities to abuse—because of its demoralizing influence upon society through these abuses—because of its impoverishing operations upon the states and communities that tolerate its continuance,* that I am a candid and fearless advocate, in my political relations, of a state constitutional termination of it by a gradual approach . . . predestinating some ultimate day, when both the master and the slave would be prepared for it.

But in the second place, as Paul once affirmed of a certain class of "all things," so I affirm of slavery in the present day. "All things," said he, "are lawful for me, but all things are not expedient." —While, then, I affirm the conviction that the relation of master and slave, by the providence and law of God, is, in certain cases and conditions, morally right, I also affirm the conviction that *in this age and in this country it is not expedient.* Of the sincerity of this conviction the best proof that I can give is, that many years since, I advised the emancipation of a number of slaves that would have come to me by inheritance, and who, consequently, were set *free* from slavery. So that I have set free from slavery every human being that came in any way under my influence or that was my property.

• • • • • • • • • • •

In the third place, also, we conclude, that *no Christian community can religiously make the simple relation of master and slave a subject of discipline or a term of communion.* In other words, no man can be censured simply for being a master, or for holding a person in servitude who was providentially born in slavery according to the constitution and laws of the state which gave him birth.

• • • • • • • • • • •

To enforce this conclusion is the sole object of this series of essays. We said, at first, that if we were true to our principles, we could not, for any difference of opinion on this subject, be alienated into two parties. We now feel confident that, under the divine blessing, we shall in this, as on other subjects, bear with one another and preserve unity of spirit in the bonds of Christian peace.

In doing this we will mutually influence each other. Those at the North will influence those at the South, and those at the South will influence those at the North; and thus our sectional aberrations and prejudices will be worn off by the friction of brotherly kindness and love.

•••••••••••

These propositions, with the documentary evidence accompanying them in our essays, we submit to the religious considerations and examination of all the holy brethren who love the peace and prosperity of the kingdom of our Lord and Saviour Jesus Christ, with our most affectionate regard for them and our ardent desires that they may be able to maintain unity of spirit and holy co-operation in the bonds of Christian peace and love.

A.C.

1846

Between 1836 and 1846, at a time when Horace Mann was campaigning for public schools, Alexander Campbell became a leading supporter of the cause. This selection contains excerpts from Campbell's address on "Universal Common School Education" given to the students of Bethany College at commencement, July 4, 1846. (From *The Millennial Harbinger*, Series III, Vol. III, July, 1846, pp. 400-411).

On Support for Public Schools

What education is, and who should participate in it; whether it should be universal or partial, are indeed the peculiar themes of the present century. And, young gentlemen, this leads me to address you specially on the part you should act in the pending controversy. . . .

You must prove . . . that the *wealth* of a community, its entire wealth, personal and real, is but the embodiment of its science, industry and virtue . . . and those arts that minister to (man's) daily comforts by supplying him with all the implements and instruments essential to the maintaining of the social state and the fruition of social life. And these I affirm he can neither possess nor enjoy without schools and colleges and the provisions necessary to their establishment and continuance.

But this is only one reason why common schools and colleges should be publicly and liberally supported. Another reason is, the *safety* of the state. Education, in its proper import, not only enlightens the understanding, but it also forms the conscience and humanizes the heart. Neither wars nor prison-ships, neither jails nor workhouses, neither laws nor civil magistrates can secure the person, the family, or the fortune of a good man from the assaults of the malignant and the wicked. This is the province of education.

There yet remains a third topic of argument which must not be omitted in every efficient appeal in favor of universal common school education. The Bible is a *written* communication from Heaven to man, and must be *read* in order to be understood, believed and obeyed. Of what use is the art of writing or the art of printing without the art of reading?

If, then, the *wealth*, the *safety*, and the *eternal happiness* of a people depend upon education. . . is it not the paramount duty of every individual member of the community to advocate, and, as efficiently as possible, to plead the cause of universal education? And is it not the first duty of a civilized government to provide for, and to carry out an adequate and an efficient system of common school education at the public expense?

On every proper occasion you will lift up your voice and give your support in favor of universal common school education as the only solid basis of a nation's wealth, the only invincible palladium of its safety, and the only enduring charter of its independence, prosperity, and happiness.

1848

Alexander Campbell's "Address on War" is, in reality, a magnificent "Address on Peace." Given to the Lyceum at Wheeling, Virginia (now West Virginia) in 1848 some three months after the close of the highly unpopular Mexican War, it caused widespread discussion both within and without the church. Delivered, also, at a time when an increasing number of persons were advocating force of arms as a means of solving the national issues of states' rights, slavery, and economic development, the address had added significance. Only a few short years later came the War Between the States, confirming Campbell's worst fears. (From *Popular Lectures and Addresses*, pp. 342-366).

Address on War

Has one Christian nation a right to wage war against another Christian nation?

On propounding to myself, and much more to you, my respected auditors, this momentous question, so affecting the reputation and involving the destiny of our own country and that of the Christian world, I confess that I rather shrink from its investigation than approach it with full confidence in my ability to examine it with that intelligence and composure so indispensable to a satisfactory decision. With your indulgence, however, I will attempt, if not to decide the question, at least to assist those who, like myself, have often, and with intense interest, reflected on the desolations and horrors of war, as indicated in the sacrifice of human life, the agonies of surviving relatives, the immense expenditures of a people's wealth, and the inevitable deterioration of public morals, invariably attendant on its existence and career.

•••••••••••

To apply these preliminary remarks to the question of this evening, it is important to note with particular attention the popular terms in which me have expressed it,— viz.: —

"Has one Christian nation a right to wage war against another Christian nation?"

We have prefixed no epithet to *war* or to *right*, while we have to the word *nation*. We have not defined the *war* as *offensive* or *defensive*. We have not defined the *right* as *human* or *divine*. But we have chosen, from the custom of the age, to prefix *Christian* to *nation*.

•••••••••••

But we must inquire into the appropriateness of the term *Christian* prefixed to *nation*—for popular use has so arranged these terms; and the controversy, either expressly or impliedly, as now-a-days occasionally conducted in this country, is, Has one *Christian* nation a right to wage war against another *Christian* nation? But, as we assume nothing, we must ask the grave and somewhat startling question—Is there a *Christian* nation in the world? or have we a definite idea of a *Christian* nation?

•••••••••••

The American nation, *as a nation*, is no more in spirit Christian than were Greece or Rome when the Apostle planted churches in Corinth, Athens, or in the metropolis of the empire, with Caesar's household in it. Roman policy, valor, bravery, gallantry, chivalry, are of as much praise, admiration and glory, in Washington and London, as they were in the very centre of the pagan world in the days of Julius or Augustus Caesar.

96

•••••••••••

Having, then, no Christian nation to wage war against another Christian nation, the question is reduced to a more rational and simple form, and I trust it will be still more intelligible and acceptable in this form—viz. *Can Christ's kingdom or church in one nation wage war against his kingdom or church in another nation?*

•••••••••••

But I will be told that this form of the question does not meet the exact state of the case, as now impinging the conscience of very many good men. While they will, with an emphatic *No,* negative the question as thus stated, they will in another form propound their peculiar difficulty: —"Suppose," say they, "England proclaims war against our nation, or that our nation proclaims war against England: have we a *right,* as *Christian men,* to volunteer, or enlist, or, if drafted, to fight against England? Ought our motto to be, 'Our country, right or wrong'? Or has our government a *right* to compel us to take up arms?"

•••••••••••

This simplifies the question and levels it to the judgment of all. It is this: —Has the Author and Founder of the Christian religion enacted war, or has he made it lawful and right for the subjects of his government to go to war against one another? Or, has he made it right for them to go to war against any nation, or for any national object, at the bidding of the present existent political authorities of any nation in Christendom?

The question is not, whether, under the new administration of universe, Christian communities have a right to wage war, in its common technical sense, against other communities. But the question is, May a Christian community, or the members of it, in their individual capacities, take up arms at all, whether aggressively or defensively, in any national conflict? We might, as before alleged, dispense with the words *aggressive* or *defensive;*

97

for a mere grammatical, logical or legal quibble will make any war either aggressive or defensive, just as the whim, caprice or interest of an individual pleases.

But the great question is, *Can an individual, not a public functionary, morally do that in obedience to his Government which he cannot do in his own case? . . .* Now, as we all, in our political relations to the government of our country, occupy positions at least inferior to that which a bond-servant holds towards his master, we cannot of right, as Christian men, obey the POWERS THAT BE in any thing not in itself justifiable by the written law of the Great King—our liege Lord and Master, Jesus Christ. Indeed, we may advance in all safety one step further, if it were necessary, and affirm that a Christian man can never, of right, be compelled to do that for the state, in defense of state rights, which he cannot of right do for himself in defense of his personal rights.

•••••••••••

The maxims of the Great Teacher and Supreme Philanthropist are, one would think, to be final and decisive on this great question. The Great Lawgiver addresses his followers in two very distinct respects: first, in reference to their duties to him and their own profession, and then in reference to their civil rights, duties and obligations.

So far as any indignity was offered to them or any punishment inflicted upon them as his followers, or for his *name's sake*, they were in no way to resent it. But in their civil rights he allows them the advantages of the protection of civil law, and for this cause enjoins upon them the payment of all their political dues, and to be subject to every ordinance of many of a purely civil nature, not interfering with their obligations to him.

•••••••••••

But as respects the life peculiar to a soldier, or the prosecution of a political war, they had no commandment. On the contrary, they were to live peaceable with all men to the full extent of their power. Their sovereign

Lord, the King of nations, is called "THE PRINCE OF PEACE." How, then, could a Christian soldier, whose "*shield*" was faith, whose "*helmet*" was the hope of salvation, whose "*breastplate*" was righteousness, whose "*girdle*" was truth, whose "*feet were shod* with the preparation of the gospel of peace," and whose "*sword*" was that fabricated by the Holy Spirit, even "*the Word of God,*"—I say, how could such a one enlist to fight the battles of a Caesar, a Hannibal, a Tamerlane, a Napoleon, or even a Victoria?

Jesus said, "All that take the sword shall perish by the sword." An awful warning! All that take it to support religion, it is confessed, have fallen by it; but it may be feared that it is not simply confined to that; for may I not ask the pages of universal history, have not all the nations created by the sword finally fallen by it? Should any one say, "Some few of them yet stand," we respond, All that have fallen also stood for a time; and are not those that now stand tottering just at this moment to their over throw? We have no doubt, it will prove in the end that nations and states founded by the sword shall fall by the sword.

●●●●●●●●●●

That the genius and spirit of Christianity, as well as the letter of it, are admitted, on all hands, to be decidedly "peace on earth, and good will among men," needs no proof to any one that has ever read the volume that contains it.

But if any one desires to place in contrast the gospel of Christ and the genius of war, let him suppose the chaplain of an army addressing the soldier on the eve of a great battle, on performing faithfully their duty, from such passages as the following:

—"Love your enemies; bless them that curse you; do good to them that hate you, and pray for them that despitefully use you and persecute you: that you may be the children of your Father in heaven, who makes his sun to rise upon the evil and the good, and sends his rain upon the just and the unjust." Again, in our civil relations:

99

—"Recompense no man evil for evil." "As much as lieth in you, live peaceably with all men." "Dearly beloved, avenge not yourselves; but rather give place to wrath." "If thine enemy hunger, feed him; if he thirst, give him drink." "Be not overcome of evil; but overcome evil with good." Would any one suppose that he had selected a text suitable for the occasion? How would the commander-in-chief have listened to him? With what spirit would his audience have immediately entered upon an engagement? These are questions which every man must answer for himself, and which every one can feel much better than express.

•••••••••••

Nothing, it is alleged, more tends to weaken the courage of a conscientious soldier than to reflect upon the originating causes of wars and the objects for which they are prosecuted. These, indeed, are not always easily comprehended. Many wars have been prosecuted, and some have been terminated after long and protracted efforts, before the great majority of the soldiers themselves, on either side, distinctly understood what they were fighting for. Even in our own country, a case of this sort has, it is alleged, very recently occurred. If, it is presumed, the true and proper causes of most wars were clearly understood, and the real design for which they are prosecuted could be clearly and distinctly apprehended, they would, in most instances, miscarry for the want of efficient means of a successful prosecution.

•••••••••••

War is not now, nor was it ever, a process of justice. It never was a test of truth—a criterion of right. It is either a mere game of chance, or a violent outrage of the strong upon the weak. Need we any other proof that a Christian people can in no way whatever countenance a war as a proper means of redressing wrongs, of deciding justice, or of settling controversies among nations? . . .

But to the common mind, as it seems to me, the most convincing argument against a Christian becoming a

100

soldier may be drawn from the fact that he fights against an innocent person—I say an innocent person, so far as the cause of the war is contemplated. The men that fight are not the men that make the war. Politicians, merchants, knaves and princes cause or make the war, declare the war, and hire men to kill for them those that may be hired on the other side to thwart their schemes of personal and family aggrandizement. The soldiers on either side have no enmity against the soldiers on the other side, because with them they have no quarrel. Had they met in any other field, in their citizen dress, other than in battle-array, they would, most probably, have not only inquired after the welfare of each other, but would have tendered to each other their assistance if called for.

•••••••••••

For my own part, and I am not alone in this opinion, I think that the moral desolations of war surpass even its horrors. And amongst these, I do not assign the highest place to the vulgar profanity, brutality and debauchery of the mere soldier, the professional and licensed butcher of mankind. . . . And were it not for the infatuation of public opinion and popular applause, I would place him, as no less to be condemned, beside the vain and pompous volunteer, who for his country, "right or wrong," hastens to the theatre of war for the mere plaudits of admiring multitudes, ready to cover himself with glory, because he has aided an aspirant to a throne or paved the way to his own election to reign over an humbled and degraded people.

•••••••••••

The pulpit, too, must lend its aid in cherishing the delusion. There is not unfrequently heard a eulogium on some fallen hero—some church-service for the mighty dead; thus desecrating the religion of the Prince of Peace, by causing it to minister as the handmaid of war. Not only are prayers offered up by pensioned chaplains on both sides of the field, even amid the din of arms, but, Sabbath after Sabbath, for years and years, have the pulpits on one side of a sea or river, and those on the other side, resounded with prayers for the success of rival armies, as if God could hear them both, and make each triumphant over the other, guiding and commissioning swords and bullets to the heads and hearts of their respective enemies!

But how are all national disputes to be settled? Philosophy, history, the Bible, teach that all disputes, misunderstandings, alienations are to be settled, heard, tried, adjudicated by impartial, that is, by disinterested, umpires. No man is admitted to be a proper judge in his own case. Wars never make amicable settlements, and seldom, if ever, just decisions of points at issue. We are obliged to offer preliminaries of peace at last. Nations must meet by their representatives, stipulate and restipulate, hear and answer, compare and decide.

In modern times we terminate hostilities by a treaty of peace. We do not make peace with powder and lead. It is done by reason, reflection and negotiation. Why not employ these at first? But it is alleged that war has long been, and must always be . . . the last argument of those in power. For ages a father Inquisitor was the strong argument for orthodoxy; but light has gone abroad, and he has lost his power. Illuminate the human mind on this subject also, create a more rational and humane public opinion, and wars will cease.

But it is alleged, all will not yield to reason and justice. There must be compulsion. Is war, then, the only compulsory measure? Is there no legal compulsion? Must all personal misunderstandings be settled by the sword?

Why not have a *by-law-established* umpire? Could not a united national court be made as feasible and as practicable as a United States court? Why not, as often proposed, and as eloquently, ably and humanely argued, by the advocates of peace, have a congress of nations and a high court of nations for adjudicating and terminating all international misunderstandings and complaints, redressing and remedying all wrongs and grievances?

•••••••••••

To sum up the whole, we argue—

1. The right to take away the life of the murderer does not of itself warrant war, inasmuch as in that case none but the guilty suffer, whereas in war the innocent suffer not only with, but often without, the guilty. The guilty generally make war, and the innocent suffer from its consequences.

2. The right given to the Jews to wage war is not vouchsafed to any other nation, for they were under a theocracy, and were God's sheriff to punish nations: consequently no Christian can argue from the wars of the Jews in justification or in extenuation of the wars of Christendom. The Jews had a Divine precept and authority: no existing nation can produce such a warrant.

3. The prophecies clearly indicate that the Messiah himself would be "The Prince of Peace," and that under his reign "wars should cease," and "nations study it no more."

4. The gospel, as first announced by the angels, is a message which results in producing "peace on earth and good will among men."

5. The precepts of Christianity positively inhibit war—by showing that "wars and fightings come from men's lusts" and evil passions, and by commanding Christians to "follow peace with all men."

6. The beatitudes of Christ are not pronounced on patriots, heroes and conquerors, but on "peace-makers," on whom is conferred the highest rank and title in the universe: —"Blessed are the PEACE-MAKERS, for they shall be called THE SONS OF GOD."

7. The folly of war is manifest in the following particulars:

1st. It can never be the criterion of justice or a proof of right.

2nd. It can never be a satisfactory end of the controversy.

3rd. Peace is always the result of negotiation, and treaties are its guarantee and pledge.

103

8. The wickedness of war is demonstrated in the following particulars:

1st. Those who are engaged in killing their brethren, for the most part, have no personal cause of provocation whatever.

2nd. They seldom, or never, comprehend the right or the wrong of the war. They, therefore, act without the approbation of conscience.

3rd. In all wars the innocent are punished with the guilty.

4th. They constrain the soldier to do for the state that which, were he to do it for himself, would, by the law of the state, involve forfeiture of his life.

5th. They are the pioneers of all other evils to society, both moral and physical. . . . With Franklin I, therefore, conclude, "There never was a *good* war, or a *bad* peace."

No wonder, then, that for two or three centuries after Christ all Christians refused to bear arms. So depose Justin Martyr, Tatian, Clement of Alexandria, Tertullian, Origen, etc.

In addition to all these considerations, I further say, were I not a Christian, as a political economist, even, I would plead this cause. Apart from the mere claims of humanity, would urge it on the ground of sound national policy.

Give me the money that has been spent in wars, and I will clear up every acre of land in the world that ought to be cleared—drain every marsh—subdue every desert—fertilize every mountain and hill—and convert the whole earth into a continuous series of fruitful fields, verdant meadows, beautiful villas, hamlets, towns, cities. . . . I would found, furnish and endow as many schools, academies and colleges, as would educate the whole human race,—would build meeting-houses, public halls, lyceums, and furnish them with libraries adequate to the wants of a thousand millions of human beings.

Beat your swords into ploughshares, your spears into pruning hooks; convert your warships into missionary packets, your arsenals and munitions of war into Bibles, school-books, and all the appliances of literature, science and art. . . . All this being done, I would doubtless have a surplus for some new enterprises.

•••••••••••

We have all a deep interest in the question; we can all do something to solve it; and it is every one's duty to do all the good he can. We must create a public opinion on this subject. We should inspire a pacifist spirit, and urge on all proper occasions the chief objections to war.

Let every one, then, who fears God and loves man, put his hand to the work; and the time will not be far distant when

> "No longer hosts encountering hosts
> Shall crowds of slain deplore:
> They'll hang the trumpet in the hall,
> And study war no more."

1849

The question of forming a responsible general convention came to a head in the early spring of 1849. A meeting held at Lexington, Kentucky at the time of the Campbell-Rice debate in 1843 and the formation of the American Christian Bible Society by D. S. Burnet in 1845, forced the issue. Several states (for example, Indiana and Kentucky) had already taken the initiative and formed regional associations. Campbell at last gave the signal for a general convention. The selections which follow brought action after seven years of discussion. (From *The Millennial Harbinger*, Series III, Vol. VI, No. V, May, 1849, pp. 271-273 and Series III, Vol. VI, No. VIII, August, 1849, pp. 475-476).

On Calling a General Convention
Church Organization—No. IV
(May, 1849)

Christian faith, worship and discipline, or what we have designated under the great categories of faith, piety and morality, we regard as matters of Divine revelation and Divine authority, already enacted and sanctioned under the broad seal of Father, Son and Holy Spirit, to which nothing is to be added and from which nothing is to be subtracted, by any synod, council, or conventional meeting whatsoever. We would, according to our taste, move an amendment of the designation of one of the great items as equally scriptural but more graphical, and read it *faith, piety* and *humanity*. These are topics beyond the tribunals of earth, whether ecclesiastical or political.

Baptist associations, Christian conferences of the elders and messengers of the Christian communities spread over certain districts, have been, under various modifications, congenial with our age and country, and adapted to the wants of the people. Their whole moral or ecclesiastic authority is purely conventional, and depending on covenanted stipulations which have but the sanction of a solemn agreement amongst the churches of a given district. These covenants or constitutions have, of course, no other authority than the voluntary agreement of the parties or churches entering into them. But like all other covenants, are morally binding in the fair construction of their respective items or articles of agreement.

•••••••••••

Reformation and annihilation are not with me now, as formerly, convertible or identical terms. We want occasional, if not stated, deliberative meetings on questions of expediency in adaptation to the ever changing fortune and character of society.

•••••••••••

It is not expedient, nor is it necessary, were we competent to the task, to go into a specification of all the objects that may legitimately and advantageously come before such meetings and conferences. The public press, . . . religious tracts, and moral agencies of every sort necessary or favorable to the prosperity of the churches of Christ and to the conversion of the world, Jew and Gentile, are probably the objects which might advantageously claim a sort of general superintendency, either by committees raised for the purpose or at the general annual meetings of these local or state associations.

•••••••••••

If our brethren will, in moderate size, forward their objections, approval or emendations by letter we will despatch the matter with all speed and concur with them in the call of a general meeting in Cincinnati, Lexington, Louisville or Pittsburgh.

A. C.

Convention
(August, 1849)

I am of opinion that a Convention, or general meeting, of the churches of the Reformation is a very great desideratum. Nay, I will say further, that it is all important to the cause of reformation. I am also of opinion that Cincinnati is the proper place for holding such Convention. But the questions are—*How shall such Convention be obtained, when shall it be held, and for what purposes?* These I cannot more than *moot*, or propound. I must, however, to suggest considerations to our brethren, say that it should not be a Convention of Book-makers or of Editors, to concoct a great book concern; but a Convention of messengers (i.e. delegates) of churches, selected and constituted such by the churches—one from every church, if possible, or if impossible, one from a district, or some definite number of churches. It is not to be composed of a few self-appointed messengers, or of messengers from one, two, or three districts, or States, but a *general* Convention. I know that neither wisdom nor piety are rated by numbers; still in the multitude of counsellors there is more general safety, and more confidence than in a few.

The purposes of such a primary convention are already indicated by the general demand for a more efficient and Scriptural organization—for a more general and efficient co-operation in the Bible cause, in the Missionary cause, in the Education cause.

A.C.

108

1849

At the close of the year 1849 Campbell gave the opening address in a study course held in Louisville, Kentucky and entitled "On the Amelioration of the Social State." In reading the address we are astonished to discover that his message is a plea for the recognition of the equality of women in society and a demand for their full education. (From *Popular Lectures and Addresses*, pp. 47-72).

On Women's Rights

These are the two superlative agencies in the amelioration of the state; they are woman and the Bible; or if it pleases to make but one out of two, it is *the Bible in the hand and heart of woman*.

Woman, with me, is to society what the spirit is to the body; for as the body without the spirit is dead, society without woman is dead also. She is then the quickening, animating, conservative element of society.

Now, her intellectual and moral culture, her elevation to her own proper rank, which is not to sit at the *foot*, but to stand by the *side*, of man, is of supreme importance to the State, to the Church, to the world and to the amelioration of the social system. But this subject has never yet taken hold of the head, the heart or the hand of man in the ratio of its importance; because, perhaps, the power of women for good or evil, for weal or for woe, has not yet appeared in its full proportions to the mental vision of even the sages and the learned of our race.

But what shall I say of the illustrious women of modern Europe, whose noble deeds, whose splendid follies, whose heroic achievements, whose mighty genius or whose public virtues have thrown a lustre on almost all the principal kingdoms of Europe? Time would fail me to tell of Margaret, Queen of Denmark ... of Margaret of Valois, mother of Henry IV, an authoress, a poetess, a queen—of another Margaret, mother of Henry VII, a patroness of learning, a founder of two colleges, although allied and related to thirty kings and queens, who spent her leisure hours not in courtly pastimes, but in translating from the French such pious books as A Kempis on Imitating Christ—of Maria Theresa, Empress Queen of Hungary, daughter of Charles VI, whose brilliant achievements and whose varied fortunes astonished Europe for forty years—of her daughter Marie Antoinette, Archduchess of Austria and Queen of France, wife of the unfortunate Louis.

I again repeat, time would fail me to tell of the Catharines of France and Russia—the Elizabeths, the Marys, the Annes of England, and a thousand other noble and illustrious names. But I will be asked, Why enumerate so many of regal dignity, of high and elevated place, of illustrious fortune, in exemplifying the power of women? Because, I answer, amongst these we have the best educated of the sex—those invested with the most ample means of showing off to advantage the leading attributes of female character, and those whose deeds are best known in human history. How much more familiar to the million are Josephine, Maria Louisa, Anne Boleyn, Joan of Arc, Lady Jane Grey and the present Victoria, than females of less conspicuous station!

Our own times, alike removed from the ages of superstition and romance, furnish clearer, more striking, richer and more varied examples, not merely of her power to attain to eminence, but of her successful competition in general literature, science, and in the fine arts of poetry, music, painting, and of living well.

I need not speak of the celebrity of Miss Edgeworth as a writer of moral tales; of Miss Baille as a tragedian; of Madame de Stael as a miscellaneous writer of much wit and vivacity; of Miss Martineau as a tourist; of Mrs. Bowdler as a moralist; and of Miss Sedgwick as a moral instructor. These are not our best models of female excellence even in the didactic arts. Nor need I refer to the celebrity of Mrs. Hemans, now commensurate with English literature; nor to that of Mrs. Sigourney, commensurate with our own; nor to the miscellaneous and moral productions of Mrs. Hannah More, of Miss Beecher, all excellent in their kind. These are becoming as familiar in our country as weekly visitors or household words. They, indeed, are all honorable vouchers of what woman might be under a more philosophic, rational and moral system of education; and, together with a thousand names of equal renown, show that the female mind only needs the proper appliances of good education to shine with a lustre, on a general scale, transcending far the humble standards fixed for it in ages, we hope, forever past.

Society is not yet fully civilized. It is only beginning to be. Things are in process, in progress to another age—a golden—a millennial—a blissful period in human history. Selfishness, violence, inordinate ambition, revenge, duelling, even tyranny, oppression and cruelty, are yet exerting a pernicious influence in society. These are the real drawbacks on human happiness—the loud calls on genuine philanthropy. Woman, I believe, is destined to be the great agent in this grandest of all human enterprises— an effort to advance society to the acme of its most glorious destiny on earth.

Who is it, then, who desires a deep and more thorough reformation of public manners and customs, or who is it that seeks for social pleasures of the highest earthly order, and would advance the amelioration of the social state to the highest point within the grasp of rational or religious anticipation? Let him turn his attention to more rational, scientific, liberal and moral education of woman. Let him bear in mind that she must take the precedence as the most puissant leader in every work of moral reform in society. Hers is the delightful task, as well as the sovereign power, to mould human nature after a divine model. She sows the seed, she plants the germs of human goodness and human greatness. She infixes the generous purpose, the salutary and noble principles in the youthful heart. She makes the men and women of future times, and shapes the character and destinies of posterity to the third, and to the fourth, and sometimes to the tenth generation. Ought not, then, every patriot, every philanthropist, every good citizen, every Christian in the land to rally all his forces, to summon all his energies, to co-operate in the great cause of female education? It is not the education of the daughters of the affluent and honorable only, or chiefly, of which we speak—it is the education of all—it is common, it is universal female education, and to a more liberal extent than has yet been imagined—for which we speak, when we plead for that female education indispensable to the full and proper amelioration of the social state.

Individual, family or national wealth never can be more advantageously appropriated, than in the mental and moral education of all the sons and daughters of the States. We owe it, then, to ourselves, to our children, to our country, to the world, to bestir ourselves in this most useful, honorable and beneficent of mortal undertakings. Let us, then, awaken to our responsibilities, and to our power of blessing others, and of being blessed, and place our energies and our influence, along with our other means, on the side of women's high advancement in all the paths of literature and science, of religion and morality. Then must we greatly enhance and sweeten the charms of home—of the social hearth—the domestic circle—the city—the church—the world.

1850

Campbell's views on capital punishment were formed over a five-year period. They appeared as short essays in *The Millennial Harbinger* beginning in September, 1845 and ended with the essay appearing in October, 1850. For the purpose of continuity they appear together in an essay entitled "Is Capital Punishment Sanctioned by Divine Authority?" from which the following selections are taken. (From *Popular Lectures and Addresses*, pp. 311-341).

On Capital Punishment

We live in the midst of a great moral revolution. Opinions held sacred by our fathers, usages consecrated by the devotion of ages, institutions venerated by the most venerable of mankind are now subjected to the same cold, rigid analysis, and made to pass through the same unsparing ordeal, to which the most antiquated errors and the most baseless hypotheses of the most reckless innovators are now so unmercifully doomed. Few, indeed, of the most popular theories of the pagan schools on the great subject of man's social and moral relations, have, when cast into this fiery furnace, like Shadrach, Meshach and Abed-nego, come out unscathed.

•••••••••••

Since the days of Plato, men have conceived republics. They have invented new orders of society, new theories of socialism, and new names for things. But these are mere demonstrations of human weaknesses and of human skepticism. The Bible has sanctioned republics, and commonwealths and kingdoms, without affixing any peculiar name to them. It prescribes no form of human government, because no one form of government would suit all the countries, climes and people of the earth. But the Bible, in the name and by the authority of its Author, demands of all persons in authority that they dispense justice to all. . . .

In the freedom of debate, and in harmony with that spirit of innovation of which we have just spoken, a question has been mooted, and is now before the American public a matter of very grave discussion. A question, too, than which, in my humble judgment, no one pertaining to this life is worthy of a more profound deliberation, nor whose decision is fraught with more fearful and important results, affecting the whole community, involving the foundation of civil government, all the fixtures of society, the extent of all earthly sovereignty, and all the principles of international law, commerce and responsibility. That question is propounded in the solemn interrogatory, IS CAPITAL PUNISHMENT SANCTIONED BY DIVINE AUTHORITY? or, in other words, *Has man a right to take away the life of man on any account whatever?*

If he have not a divine right, I frankly admit that he has no human right—no warrant or authority derived from man—that will authorize such a solemn and fearful act. Though we should not, in the first instance, take into account the consequences of any decision, as having direct authority in influencing our reasonings upon the question, still it is important that we have some respect for them as arguments and incentives to a calm, discreet and patient investigation of the premises from which are to be adduced conclusions so deeply involving the interests of the world.

• • • • • • • • • • •

But, further, if man has not the right to kill, nations have no right to go to war in any case, or for any purpose whatever. We argue that whatever power a Government has is first found in the people; that men cannot innocently or rightfully do that conventionally, or in states, which they cannot do in their individual capacities. True, when a Government is organized, the citizens or subjects of it cannot use or exercise the powers to legislate, to judge, to punish, which, by the social compact, they have, for wise purposes, surrendered or transferred to the Government. Still, the fundamental fact must not be lost sight of—that *nations have the right to do those things only which every individual man had a right to do anterior to the national form of society.* If, then, man had not originally a right to kill him who killed his brother, society never could, but from a special law of the Creator, have such a right. And, such, we may hereafter show, was originally the divine law. The natural reason of man, or a divine law, enacted that the blood of the murdered should be avenged by the blood of the murderer, and that the brother of the murdered was pre-eminently the person to whom belonged the right of avenging his blood.

Wars are either defensive or aggressive. But, in either point of view, they are originated and conducted on the assumption that man has a right, for just cause, to take away the life of man. For it needs no argument to convince any one, however obtuse, that man cannot rightfully kill a thousand or a million of persons, if he cannot lawfully kill one! I wonder not, then, that peace-men are generally, if not universally, in favor of the total abolition of capital punishment.

••••••••••

Some of the most dogmatical of the new schools of philosophy assume that the sole end of punishment is the reformation of the offender; that the murderer must be sent to a school of repentance and be better educated, and, when properly instructed and honorably graduated, he shall have his passport into the confidence of society, and be permitted to develop himself in the midst of more

115

favorable circumstances. Such is one of the most popular substitutes for capital punishment.

We agree with those who affirm that punishments ought, in all cases, to be enacted and enforced with a special regard to the reformation of transgressors; but we cannot say with an *exclusive* regard. Emphatic and special, but not *exclusive*, regard, should be shown to the reformation of the criminal. There must also be a special and a supreme regard to the safety of the state, and the protection of the innocent and unoffending. The laws of every civilized community should unite as far as possible the reformation of the offender with the safety of the state.

But how these two may be best secured, is a matter not yet agreed. A sentence of perpetual imprisonment is no guarantee of protection or safety to the state. The sentence, in the first place, may not be executed. It seldom is, in the case of persons holding high places in society. Governors sometimes reprieve. But, further, it is not guaranteed that the monster who has been guilty of one murder may not murder some of his attendants or fellow-prisoners in hope of escape, or that he may not fire his prison or in some way elope. He may be confined for life, and yet may again perpetrate the same foul crime. Are there not numerous instances of this kind on record?

And, strange as it may seem, we affirm the conviction that the certainty of death is, upon all the premises, the most efficient means of reformation. When . . . the *malignant and wicked murderer* has been tried, convicted and sentenced to die after the lapse of so many days or weeks, when all hope of pardon is forever gone, then evangelical instruction is incomparably more likely to effect a change than are the chances of a long or short life within the walls of a penitentiary. It is, therefore, I must think, more rational and humane, whether we consider the safety of the state or the happiness of the individual, to insist that the sentence of death be promptly and firmly executed.

•••••••••••

But we can very sincerely sympathize with many good men in their aversion to capital punishment for any other crime than murder. Indeed, much of the excitement and indignation against capital punishment arises from two sources: —the many crimes that have been judged worthy of death; and the fact that the innocent sometimes suffer while the guilty escape. In noticing the various topics from which men reason against the justice of demanding life for life, our design is to show how doubtful and inconclusive all mere human reasonings and statutes on this subject must be, rather than to enter into a full investigation of all that may be alleged from these sources of reason and argumentation.

We cheerfully admit that our criminal code is not in unison with the spirit of the age, nor with the presiding genius of European and American civilization. Christian justice, humanity and mercy have, indeed, in some countries, and in one more than in our own, greatly modified and improved political law and political justice.

●●●●●●●●●●●

We advocate a discriminating tariff of penalties and punishments, not for the sake of revenue alone, but for the sake of protecting innocence and virtue. We have no faith either in the justice or expediency of a horizontal tariff, awarding one and the same punishment to each and to every one of a hundred crimes. We would not hang one man for stealing a shilling, and inflict the same punishment for treason, sacrilege, rape or murder. We believe in the scriptural phrases, "worthy of stripes," "worthy of a sorer punishment," and "worthy of death." These forms of speech occur in both Testaments, but more frequently in the New than in the Old. They are phrases from which a sound and irrefutable argument in support of capital punishment may be deduced, and which no one opposed to it will dare on any occasion to employ.

●●●●●●●●●●●

The penal code of every community should be an index of its moral sense and of its moral character. It ought to be regarded as a licensed exposition of its views upon the comparative criminality and malignity of every action affecting the life, the liberty, the character or the prosperity of its citizens, —a polished mirror from which may be reflected upon its own citizens and upon the world at large a nation's intelligence, moral taste and moral excellency. Should it affix the same punishment to various and numerous offenses, irrespective of their grade in criminality, it will confound and bewilder the moral perceptions of the people, and exhibit to the world a very fallacious test of the comparative atrocity and malignity of human actions.

••••••••••

From such considerations and reasonings as these, we would advocate a scale of punishments in harmony with the most correct views of the criminality and wickedness of human actions, rising up to capital punishment only in the case of willful and deliberate murder, not to be extenuated in any case by passion, intemperance, or any temptation whatsoever. To obviate the exception not unfrequently taken to capital punishment on the ground that sometimes the innocent may suffer while the guilty escape, might there not be such legal provisions as would prevent the possibility of any one being convicted without such strength of testimony and proof of guilt as would not leave the shadow of a doubt? We doubt not the practicability of such a provision.

••••••••••

There is not, then, a word in the Old Testament or the New inhibiting capital punishment, nor a single intimation that it should be abolished. On the contrary, reasons are given as the basis of the requisition of life for life, which never can be set aside—which are as forcible at this hour as they were in the days of Cain, Noah, Moses and Jesus Christ. We reiterate the statute with clearer conviction of its obligation and utility on every consideration of the broad, deep, solid and enduring premises on which it is founded: —"Thou shalt take (no ransom) no

118

satisfaction for the life of the murderer." —"He that sheddeth man's blood, by man shall his blood be shed; for in the image of God made he man." —"The land cannot be cleansed from blood but by the blood of him that shed it." For this purpose the magistrate is "God's minister, an avenger, to execute wrath upon him that doeth evil."

The necessity, utility and importance of capital punishment, we must regard, on the premises already considered, as unequivocally and irrefragably established, so far as divine authority can require and establish any thing.

1852

This address was presented by Campbell to a literary society of Jefferson College, Canonsburg, Pennsylvania (now Washington and Jefferson College, Washington, Pennsylvania) on the college's 50th anniversary, August 3, 1852. The selection below is from the last section of the presentation. (From *Popular Lectures and Addresses*, pp. 175-185).

On the Destiny of Our Country

Let our nation, then, be just, true and benevolent to all nations and to herself, and it will stand while time endures. The pulse of time and of human life is not merely indicative of, but absolutely dependent upon, the action of the heart. The universe was conceived and born in the bosom of absolute, eternal and immutable benevolence. Benevolence has for its sisters righteousness and truth. This being the moral character of the divine being, is immutable and eternal. On these principles our country stands; and on these principles alone she can stand, and rise, and flourish, to meet not only her own wishes and her own happiness, but the expectations and the prayers of all the great and wise and good of mankind.

Let it, then, be so established and published to the world, that we are the stern, uncompromising advocates of human rights; that America is not only "the home of the brave," but "the land of the free"; that we supremely love equal rights, and bow to no sovereignty but to that of

God and the moral sentiments; that with open arms and warm hearts me welcome to our shores the oppressed and down-trodden of all nations and languages; and that while the old world is pouring into our harbors and into our homes her ignorant, superstitious and down-trodden serfs and masses, we will, by common schools and common ministrations of benevolence, dispossess them of the demons of priestcraft and kingcraft, and show them our religion by pointing to our common schools, our common churches, our common colleges, and our common respect for the Bible, the Christian religion and its divine and glorious founder—the Supreme Philanthropist.

••••••••••

Patriotism, it is conceded, has no special place in the Christian religion. Its founder never pronounced a single sentence in commendation of it. The reason is, I presume to say, that the world was his field, and as patriotism is only an extension of the principle of selfishness, he deigned it no regard; because selfishness is now the great and damning sin of mankind. Still, the very test of morality is self-love. We are commanded to love our neighbor as we love ourselves, neither more nor less. And in his enlarged mind and heart, our neighbor is every man in the world.

Charity, it is said, begins at home, but at home it does not stay. It goes abroad, and radiates its blessings according to its strength, to the utmost domicile of man. But few men can extend their charity, in its special currency, beyond their village, their parish, or their church. Still, when the frozen Icelander or the sunburned Moor comes within our sphere of doing good, we will, as we ought, pour into his wounds and bruises the soothing and mollifying ointment of Christian benevolence. Our country, then, for the most part, engages our attention, and exhausts all our means of doing good. But in promoting its moral excellence, its wealth, its honor, its character, we increase its power and extend its means of communicating blessings which, without it, no Christian man could bestow upon his species.

The United States of America, as they grow in learning, in the arts and sciences, and in all the elements of human wealth and power, can extend blessings to many nations; indeed, to the four quarters of the world. In promoting her health, her wealth and greatness, especially that natural characteristic of a paramount regard for the freedom, amelioration, civilization, as well as the evangelization of foreign lands, we lay for her prosperity, for our own, for that of our children, for that of the human race, the most solid, substantial and enduring basis, pregnant, too, with the civilization and advancement of the great family of man. In this way, too, we secure for ourselves and for our posterity the richest inheritance which mortals can secure in heaven or on earth. If, then, as a nation and a people we stand out upon the canvas of time as the most generous, magnanimous and benevolent nation, we will, as certainly as the sun radiates and attracts, bless the nations and be blessed by them, and grow in every element and characteristic of a great, a mighty, a prosperous and a happy people.

1853

In October, 1853, Campbell addressed the annual meeting of the American Christian Missionary Society of which he had been president since its founding. In the four years of the society's existence it had sent out one missionary, James T. Barclay, to Jerusalem. The following selections are focused on an appeal to enlarge the scope of the society's work. (From *Popular Lectures and Addresses*, pp. 518-530).

On the Necessity for Missions

Beloved Brethren in the Cause of Christian Missions: —Missions and angels are coeval, inasmuch as message and messenger are correlates: the one implies the other. As message implies a messenger, so both imply two parties—one that sends and one that receives the message.

•••••••••••

So essentially diffusive and missionary is the spirit of Christianity, that all forms of it have acknowledged the duty and obligation to extend its empire and to propagate it in all lands and amongst all people. Hence, Romanists themselves, and Protestants of every name, have instituted and sustained missions, domestic and foreign, and sacrificed both property and life, to a large amount, in their endeavors to evangelize the world, by bringing it under the sceptre and the sway of the Prince of Life and Peace.

Myriads of men in the flesh will labor, in body, soul and spirit, for a lifetime, to secure temporal honors and rewards. They will imperil all that is dear to the human heart, for some imaginary gain, which, when possessed, fails to satisfy an ardent, immortal mind. But the Christian herald or missionary who, with a true heart, an enlightened zeal and untiring labor, engages in the service of the wisest, richest, noblest and most exalted potentate in the universe, and for the honor, the blessedness and the glory of his own degenerate race, to raise them from poverty, wretchedness, infamy and ruin, to glory, honor and immortality, is the noblest spectacle that earth affords or that angels have seen on this side the gates of the heavenly Jerusalem.

••••••••••

This Christian Missionary Society, my beloved brethren, we trust, originated in such conceptions as these, and from having tasted that the Lord has been gracious to us, in giving us a part in his own church, a name and a place in that Divine institution; which, in his mind, far excels and outweighs all the callings, pursuits and enterprises of this our fallen and bewildered world.

••••••••••

The commission given to the apostles embraced, as a mission-field, the whole world. "Go ye," said the great Apostle of God, "*into all the world*, and preach the gospel to every creature." Wide as humanity and enduring as time, or till every son of Adam hears the message of salvation, extends this commission in its letter, spirit and obligation. The apostles, indeed, are yet upon the earth, in their writings. Though dead, they still are preaching.

••••••••••

This missionary enterprise is, by universal concession, as well as by the oracles of God, the grand work of the age—the grand duty, privilege and honor of the church of the nineteenth century. God has by his provi-

124

dence opened up the way for us. He has given us learning, science, wealth, and knowledge of the condition of the living world—of the pagan nations, their languages, customs, rites and usages. He has given to us the earth, with all its seas, lakes, rivers and harbors. He has, in the arts and improvements of the age, almost annihilated distance and time, and by our trade and commerce we have, in his providence, arrested the attention and commanded the respect of all heathen lands, of all creeds and of all customs.

Our national flag floats in every breeze; our nation and our language command the respect, almost the homage, of all the nations and the people of the earth. God has opened the way for us—a door which no man or nation can shut. Have we not, then, as a people, a special call, a loud call, a Divine call, to harness ourselves for the work, the great work—the greatest work of man—the preaching of the gospel of eternal life to a world dead, spiritually dead, in trespasses and sins? And shall we lend to it a cold, a careless, an indifferent ear?

We have but one foreign mission-station—a station, indeed, of all others the most apposite to our profession—the ancient city of the Great King, the city of David, on the summit of the "holy hill," once the royal residence of Melchezidek, priest of the most high God—the sacred Solyma—the abode of peace. There stood the tabernacle when its peregrinations ended. There stood the temple, the golden palace which Solomon built.

•••••••••••

Jerusalem is a great centre of attraction in the eyes of all Christendom, in the esteem and admiration of all Jews and Gentiles. It will long continue to be so. The crowds of tourists—Jews, Turks, Infidels, Romanists and Protestants—that visit, sojourn and take interest in it, give it a paramount interest and claim to locate therein a herald of the original gospel and of the apostolic order of things, free from the false philosophies of an apostate Christendom. An accomplished missionary in Jerusalem, even in the private walks of life, in his daily intercourse

125

with strangers and sojourners, may sow the precious seed in many a heart, that may spring up in many a clime, and bring forth a large harvest of glory to God and happiness to man, when those who originated the mission and have sustained it shall repose with their fathers in the bosom of Abraham.

•••••••••••

But this is not the exclusive object of our zeal, ability and liberality. Jerusalem and Judea do not constitute the world, nor is our Jerusalem mission exclusively the longitude and the latitude of our missionary obligation, enterprise or benevolence. Has Africa, debased, degraded and down-trodden at home and abroad, no part in our Christian humanity and sympathy? Are we under no obligation to Africa?

•••••••••••

But these are foreign missions, and located on another continent. Have we no home mission-stations? Have we no fields to cultivate beyond the precincts of our American Zion? We *have* home missions, as well as foreign missions, and these have claims upon us. Have we made, or can we make, no provision for these? These are questions that call for our consideration; and ought we not as a brotherhood, if not as a missionary society, to give them some attention?

•••••••••••

Through the benevolence of brethren in Kentucky, there has been emancipated from slavery a colored brother, a gifted preacher of the gospel—a workman, we are informed, well qualified for such a field of labor. Bro. Ephraim A. Smith, whose praise is in all the churches, has, of his own accord and at his own expense, volunteered to visit Africa, to survey the premises in Liberia, and to return and report the condition of things there. He asks nothing from this Society in the form of pecuniary aid, nor has he ever suggested—to me, at least—a desire to be specially noticed on this occasion. Still, knowing

126

him so well and so long as I do, I conceive it my duty, before sitting down, to offer the following resolution, viz. *That Bro. Ephraim A. Smith be requested to report, at proper intervals, to the Corresponding Secretary of this Board, whatever he may deem important on the condition and prospects of Liberia in particular and of Africa in general, with special reference to the location of a missionary station in Africa, and that the prayers of the brethren, not only of this organization, but of all the brethren everywhere, be offered to the throne of grace for his safekeeping and protection. . . .*

"Now, may he that supplieth seed to the sower and bread for food, supply and multiply your seed sown, and increase the fruits of your righteousness and humanity— being enriched in every thing to all bountifulness," which will yield a rich harvest of glory to God and blessedness to man.

1854

On the occasion of the dedication of a new church building in 1854 in Wheeling, Virginia (now West Virginia), Campbell chose to deliver a stirring address on the need for and support of colleges. (From *Popular Lectures and Addresses*, pp. 291-307).

Address on Colleges

Colleges and schools of every rank are, or ought to be, founded on some great principle in human nature and in human society. They are presumed to have been, and of right ought to be, founded on a sound philosophy of man, in all his relations to society, and the universe.

•••••••••••

Thus we are led to conceive of the proper elements that enter into the constituency of a philosophical, rational and moral education.

A school is well defined to be "any establishment in which *persons* are instructed in arts, science, languages, or in any species of learning; and occasionally it merely indicates the pupils assembled for instruction." It may be a family school, an infant school, a common school, an academy, a college, or a university. But, of whatever character its subjects or its objects, its aim should be the physical, the intellectual, the moral and the religious development and culture of the pupils that compose it.

128

There are in this view of the subject two capital ideas. The first is *development*, the second is *culture*. The first supposes that in a human being there are certain organs, powers or capacities, that may be expanded, developed and corroborated to a certain maximum or extent, which will give to the subject the entire use of himself in respect to himself and to his species.

1. Physical education takes under its special surveillance and instruction the physical constitution, in all its characteristics, and sets about the scientific development and corroboration of all its organs, especially its head, heart, lungs, stomach and viscera, essential to vital action, good health and growth. It directs the character and the extent of self-denial and physical exercise essential to these ends, with the necessary attention to food and raiment.

2. Intellectual education, after giving an analysis of the intellectual powers—perception, memory, reflection, reason, imagination, abstraction—proceeds to the exercise and employment of them in the acquisition and communication of knowledge, including grammar, logic, rhetoric, oratory, taste, discussion and debate.

3. Moral culture is not the mere study of moral science. It begins with an analysis of the moral powers— the conscience, the affections, the passions, and the continual exercise of them in all the relations of life—in truthfulness, justice, honor, benevolence, humanity and mercy.

4. Religious development. Man being the subject of religious and moral obligations, he must be made to perceive, realize and acknowledge these obligations in every step of his progress in all the relations of life. The only text-book for this study and science is the Bible. It is, therefore, and ought of right to be, more or less the study of every day in every seminary of learning. It is the only proper text-book for these most essential and important of all the sciences and studies of life.

●●●●●●●●●●●

Men, and not brick and mortar, make colleges, and these colleges make men. These men make books, and these books make the living world in which we individually live, and move, and have our being. How all-important, then, that our colleges should understand and teach the true philosophy of man! They create the men that furnish the teachers of men—the men that fill the pulpit, the legislative halls, the senators, the judges and the governors of the earth.

But, as radical and most fundamental of all, we must have the true theory of education—a theory grounded in the true philosophy of man—before we can devise any system of public or private education in harmony with the genius of humanity and the wants of society. And here, again, we call attention to the importance of having the true science or theory of man before we can devise a system of instruction in accordance with the wants of the individual and of society. It has become a trite saying, that the whole man—body, soul and spirit—must be developed and educated up to the entire capacity of his nature, and with especial reference to his present, future and eternal destiny.

And at this stand-point we must congratulate ourselves that we live not merely in an age of progress, but that we have progressed so far as to ascertain, from the analytic and synthetic science of the past and the present age, that man has a purely physical, a purely intellectual and a purely moral nature, in his own proper personality. And also that these three are of necessity to be subjects of man's education from the cradle to the grave.

•••••••••••

The learned professions of all civilized communities are the benefactions of our colleges. For their endowment and support, we receive in return, as items of profit, all the wisdom and eloquence that fill the legislative halls, the courts of justice, the synagogues and temples of religion and virtue; all who learnedly minister to our wants and wishes in literature, in science, in physics and metaphysics, in the elegant and useful arts of our age and

130

country. They furnish us not only with lawyers, physicians, ministers of religion, teachers of all the sciences and arts of the living age, but, directly and indirectly, they are the fountains of all the discoveries and improvements in our country and in the present civilized world.

I know no earthly subject, no political question, so full of eloquence, so prolific in argument, and so powerful in its claims upon the patronage, the support, the liberality, of the age and of a civilized people, as these great fountains of civilization and blessings to ourselves, to our children and to the human race. All that lies between barbarism and the highest civilization, all that distinguishes the rude American Indian and the most polished citizen, the barbarian and the Christian, has been achieved by the learning, the science, the arts, the religion and the morals which colleges have nourished, cherished and imparted to the world.

1854

The student of Alexander Campbell is constantly amazed at the depth and breadth of his reading. In addition to his heavy schedule of editing, traveling, and speaking, he was able to read much of the best literature of his day. The selection which follows gives evidence of such knowledge. (From *The Millennial Harbinger*, Fourth Series, Vol. IV, No. V, May, 1854, pp. 241-254).

On Samuel Taylor Coleridge

I have recently added to my library "the complete works of Samuel Taylor Coleridge, edited by professor Shedd, in seven volumes. New York: Harper and Brothers—1853." Of course I have not read them all, nor any one volume of the seven, from cover to cover. We, now-a-days, read very few books from beginning to end. Some we read so far as to see through the whole volume. But there are some volumes so opaque, that Newton himself, with all his optics, dioptics and catoptrics, could not see through them. But such is not the character of the volumes of this pre-eminent Christian philosopher, metaphysician, critic, lecturer and poet. Few men have equaled him in any one of these professions; none has excelled him; more probably, none has equaled him in them all.

Certainly he was not addicted to swear to the dictum of any master. He thought for himself. And while he felt like a man, he thought as a sage. He was not, by profession, a theologian; yet all the theologues of Britain did homage to his genius, and none dared to contend with him in equal combat. He has greatly sustained the sound doctrine of the English hierarchy, and made sad havoc of its errors and of its hierarchical pretensions. He had pierced Unitarianism under the fifth rib, as Abner smote Asahel, or as Ehud pierced Eglon, the King of Moab.

But in every prominent position assumed by us as a people, on account of which we have been calumniated by the sectarian press, he not only sustains, but fortifies all our capital positions.

●●●●●●●●●●

It gives me pleasure to hear a voice of so much volume, pouring forth on the Island of Great Britain, in the ears of its Bishops, its Lordly Prelates and Archbishops, the honest truth, and that, too, on the text of Jeremy Taylor, its beau ideal of Episcopal grace and dignity—that our Bishops all over the West—that is, the *elders* of our churches, or presbyters, more learnedly—are severally and collectively, by Heaven's own institution, *being honest, faithful, and able men*, just as high functionaries of Almighty God and of our Lord Jesus Christ, as was Jeremy Taylor, or as are the Archbishops of York and Canterbury! This used to be called "Campbellism," some thirty years ago, but it is Coleridgism in Great Britain; and, better still, it is Paulism. Nay, it is Christ's own institution. This view, so reprobate and reprehensible in the eyes of all the *little would-be great* ecclesiastic dignitaries, from the class-leader up to Bishop Asbury, or any other dignitary in Protestantism, domestic or foreign, is the only scriptural view; and that being so, on what basis stands Roman, English and American Bishops! Mr. Coleridge, than whom, they say, there was no greater sage, philosopher, or anything else, indeed, ever born of Anglo-Saxon blood, has, we hope, set some of their minds agog, and free from all that is yet papal in Protestantism.

But to proceed—

These positions of Coleridge, and many more of the same family, more than thirty years ago, in this latitude, in the days of the Christian Baptist, were called our heresies. But a rose, under any other name, just smells as sweet. They are the rudimental truths of Christianity, and will as certainly pervade Christian society as the Bible came from God.

•••••••••••

I must confess, that the more I commune with my Bible and the great men in all the folds of the manifold flock of Christ, now extant, the more my soul is enlarged, and elevated, and encouraged in the great work we have on hand. All our capital points, on which we plead the conversion of the world, the union of the church, and the destruction of all false philosophies and false theologies, by starving them out, by letting them alone, and preaching and teaching Christ as preached and taught in the Four Gospels and Acts of Apostles, are sustained, approved, and commended by the letter and the spirit of such men as Luther and Coleridge, as Sherlock and Hooker, Fuller, Hall and Bunyan; and even the somewhat fanatical Edward Irving, George Whitfield, and John Wesley. True, some two or three of these began in the spirit and ended in the flesh. Still, they rolled the stone away from the sepulchre in which the papists had buried our Lord and sat on it, in mixed emotions and with perturbed imaginations. But here we must lay down our pen for the present, and attend to other duties.

A. C.

1858

With the January, 1858, issue of *The Millennial Harbinger*, Campbell was beginning his 35th year as an editor and publisher. In the preface to that issue he reflected upon his experience and anticipated the new year. (From *The Millennial Harbinger*, Fifth Series, Vol. I, No. 1, January, 1858, pp. 3-8).

Preface, *The Millennial Harbinger*,
January, 1858

In our present currency a *Preface* and an *Introduction*, though not exact synonyms, are synonymous in our popular style. They are, however, used as indicative of what may be expected to follow in the design and intention of a writer or speaker. But in our miscellaneous productions which are intended to keep pace with the times and the circumstances, the special and the general calls, indications, and wants of a generation or a population, unless we could foresee or anticipate the future with more than human prescience, we should not write a preface till we actually knew the whole contents of the volume.— This we cannot anticipate nor even imagine. The church and the world never stand still; they are constantly in motion forward or backward, upward or downward. Every thing in our universe is in motion. The pulse of life never stands still. Every living man is ascending or descending every moment of his existence. He is daily growing in virtue or in vice, in conformity to God or to Satan.

•••••••••

We have now been *thirty-five years* before the community as an editor, and have not failed once a month to make a visit to our constant readers during that period. This is more than half our life. Many other volumes besides these have passed through our hands during this period. These all, more or less, have been pleading the cause of ancient original Christianity. We have not labored alone, nor have we labored in vain. Whatever evil has been done is ours; whatever good has been done is the Lord's. We can, on review of all the past, say, that we have sincerely and conscientiously advocated what we have esteemed to be the truth of the Christian Religion; and, according to our conceptions opposed only the doctrines and the commandments of men, standing in contrast and in opposition to the doctrine and commandments of our Lord and his Apostles.

•••••••••

We have, from our first published sermon on the law, A. D., 1816, before the Redstone Baptist Association, till this present hour, Dec. 12th, A. D., 1857, never offered one substitute for the New Testament as a church constitution, term or terms of Christian union, communion and co-operation.

But while thus affirming we would not say that, as a Christian community—composed of all the denominational forms of Protestantism—we have, as yet, attained to perfection in our views of church co-operation. We have, indeed, said something and thought much of a more evangelical organization with special respect to a more efficient promulgation of the gospel to those outside of our communion.

•••••••••

The subject of a more effective organization is, and has been for some time past, pressed and been pressing upon our attention. We found it in our recent excursions in Illinois and Iowa, every where more less in demand, and, indeed, much needed. All societies in their incipiency, must be somewhat disciplined in the school of experience. There were some "things wanting" and for some time craved on the part of the churches planted by the apostles and their contemporary laborers. Experience of wants in almost all cases, political and religious, is more or less necessarily requisite to a proper appreciation of the supply of them, and to a proper remedy for them.

The Christian kingdom could not have been established and was not established without the aid of apostles, prophets, evangelists, pastors, and teachers. When the Lord Jesus was enthroned in the heavens, he immediately sent down to Jerusalem the Holy Spirit as the advocate of his cause and claims on the people of Israel. He being crowned Lord of all, and having received the promise of the Holy Spirit, sent him down to Jerusalem to give success to his cause and mission. We, therefore, date the origin of the Christian kingdom not from the birth of Christ in Bethlehem, but from the coronation of Jesus Christ as Lord of all. Such was the view taken of it in the beginning of our public labors, in the cause of primitive Christianity. The birth, life, miracles, teachings, preachings, sufferings, death, burial, resurrection, ascension, and coronation of Jesus Christ as Lord of all, constitute the whole materials of Christianity.

Hence the annunciation of these facts by Peter, entrusted with the keys of the kingdom of heaven—or of *the heavens*—on the first Pentecost celebrated in Jerusalem after the Lord's ascension and coronation, were made the materials of the Christian Institution—and of the gospel age or dispensation.

•••••••••••

The opening speech of the new dispensation of remedial grace and mercy was given to Peter, because he first uttered the oracle embracing the person, office, and mission of his Lord and Master, in the assertion and development of the past, that God the Father of the whole family in heaven and earth, *had constituted the same Jesus whom they had crucified "both Lord and Christ,"* or had *christened him Lord*—anointed him *sovereign Lord* of the Universe. This was, indeed, but the consummation of all that John the Baptist and the Lord Jesus during his ministry had preached, pertinent to that petition which he dictated to his disciples in what is frequently called the "Lord's prayer."

A full and satisfactory development of the Christian institution, or the kingdom of Jesus Christ, announced in the Four Gospels, depends upon a clear conception and appreciation of one petition in this prayer. This we make preparatory not only to a new volume of the M. Harbinger, but essentially preparatory to a luminous and comprehensive view of the whole Christian Revelation and the Christian church.

Epilogue

After Thomas Campbell's death in early January, 1854, Alexander's health was never the same. The father and son had worked so closely together that they had been almost as one. Campbell's major task was the completion of his work on the *Acts of the Apostles* for the American Bible Union. In his biography of Campbell, Robert Richardson states that the intense effort Campbell gave to this work and the confinement in his study for long hours during most of 1855 took its toll on his health. His friends began to notice a decline in Campbell's mental powers, a confusion regarding events of the past and strange incongruities in his articles for the *Harbinger*.

The period of Campbell's major writing was behind him. Even though he kept the management of *The Millennial Harbinger* he increasingly left the major editorial work on the magazine to Richardson, to his son-in-law William K. Pendleton, and to several other persons who served with Campbell as co-editors.

Campbell was roused to fresh efforts one final time in the need to rebuild the main building of Bethany College. A disastrous fire early on the morning of December 10, 1857 completely destroyed the college hall, together with its library and laboratories. Classes were suspended for only one day and plans were made immediately for a new building. Campbell and Pendleton were appointed by the trustees as agents to solicit resources for rebuild-

139

ing. They soon left for a tour of the East to raise funds. Upon their return home from that trip they set out within days for the South and West. By the summer of 1858 a cornerstone was laid for a fine new building but the intense efforts in money raising of the previous months left Campbell physically and emotionally spent.

News of the attack on Fort Sumter, April 22, 1860, which signaled the beginning Of the War Between the States, reached Campbell while he was engaged in a period of preaching at Charlottesville, Virginia. He left at once for his home at Bethany, noticing along the way evidence of preparation for war. In *The Millennial Harbinger* he urged a resort to arbitration as the proper method of settling the issue between the North and the South and appealed for calm and reason, but it was not to be. In 1861 Campbell found the time to edit a volume in honor of his parents, entitled *Memoirs of Elder Thomas Campbell, Together with a Brief Memoir of Mrs. Jane Campbell* (Cincinnati: H. S. Bosworth, 1861).

During the war Campbell was necessarily restricted to Bethany, but he did make occasional trips to nearby communities to speak publicly on topics related to Christian faith. He continued as president of the college in the midst of a depleted student body until a further decline in health forced him to turn his duties over to the vice-president, William K. Pendleton. On March 4, 1866 he died in the bedroom of his home at Bethany amidst family and friends, content in having served Jesus Christ as Lord and Savior and having worked as faithfully as he knew how for the furtherance of God's kingdom on earth.

Index